# MARK:
## THE SORROWFUL GOSPEL

*An Introduction
to the
Second Gospel*

John F. O'Grady

PAULIST PRESS
New York/Ramsey

N.T. - Mark - introductions

Library of Congress
Catalog Card Number: 81-82337

ISBN: 0-8091-2403-3

Published by Paulist Press
545 Island Road, Ramsey, N.J. 07446

Printed and bound in the
United States of America

# Contents

TO JOYCE S. ROMAN—
LOYAL SECRETARY,
FAITHFUL FRIEND

# Preface

People are forever asking me about the Bible. They seem to think that because a major part of my adult life has been devoted to the study of the Scriptures I know all there is to know about the Bible. My usual response is to suggest that if they are interested in the New Testament, they might begin with the Gospel of Mark, since it is the shortest Gospel, and I usually suggest that they read the Gospel in its entirety. I also recommend that if they have the time, they should take some paper and jot down what interests them as they read. Then, when they read the Gospel again, they should do the same thing and compare the notes. They usually discover that the Gospels continue to offer new insights into life and into the meaning of faith.

Certainly the above has been true for me. I believe that I know something about the Bible. I feel comfortable about a few books in the Old Testament and an equal number in the New Testament. Most of the books remain in the realm of the unknown to me even after years of study. The reason should be evident: the more I am aware of the depth of the Bible, the more I come to understand that the Bible is a mystery. We can understand something, but never understand it all.

This little book is offered to help people in their effort to read and think and pray about their faith. It is not meant to be exhaustive but rather to serve as an introduction to the general themes that run throughout Mark. I have been selective with the hope that my choice will encourage further study. I have also tried to avoid long lists of biblical references. When I thought it helpful, I have quoted the text in full. The book is not meant to be read along with the Gospel of Mark, but should be seen as an introduction to the Gospel.

After the reading has been completed, I would suggest that the reader follow the recommendations as mentioned above with regard to the actual text of Mark. In this way, my purpose will have been fulfilled.

This book is also intended to be used in introductory courses in the New Testament, since it tries to present the most recent attempts of scholarship with regard to Mark. I would hope that such an introduction would give the student of the Bible additional incentive to pursue some of the works quoted in the Bibliography.

As is true for all that I have written, most of the ideas contained herein I have learned from others. If they go unnamed, that does not mean that they are forgotten. I am particularly grateful for the scholars who have written extensively on Mark. From their work we have all gained. Since we are involved in a common pursuit of the kingdom of God, may these efforts be of help to others.

# Chapter One
# The Gospel and
## the Primitive Preaching

To the contemporary mind, documents which have their origin some two thousand years ago do not generate much enthusiasm even if those documents are the basis for faith. People listen to the readings from the New Testament and hear homilies presented, but still, for many, the writings about Jesus of Nazareth remain so much a part of the vast unknown for many Christians. They surely have their value and their effect, but it is not so evident how this is so.

To understand the writings of the New Testament demands more than just a casual listening in a church. The listeners must become readers and thinkers and also people who pray.

When Jesus was raised from the dead, God the Father gave a clear affirmation to the teachings, life and death of his Christ. As a result people could have their faith based on a sure foundation. These people, however, those who responded to Jesus, should not be considered as the greatest of theologians. They were ordinary believers limited not only in their understanding but circumscribed by the confines of first-century Palestine.

## Collections

The early followers of Jesus were Jews. "Man of Israel, hear these words" (Acts 2:22). "You know the word which he sent to Israel, preaching the good news of peace

by Jesus Christ" (Acts 10:36). They were avidly expecting
the second coming of the Lord, and while waiting they
experienced some need to preserve his teachings. In all
probability there were collections of his miracles as well as
groupings of some of his ethical teachings such as are
found in Matthew 13:31–33:

> "The kingdom of heaven is like a grain of mus-
> tard seed which a man took and sowed in his
> field; it is the smallest of seeds but when it has
> grown it is the greatest of shrubs and becomes a
> tree so that the birds of the air come and make
> nests in its branches."

> He told them another parable: "The kingdom of
> heaven is like leaven which a woman took and
> hid in three measures of meal until it was all
> leavened."

Similar collections are found in the same chapter, verses
44–48:

> "The kingdom of heaven is like treasure hidden
> in a field which a man found and covered up;
> then in his joy he goes and sells all that he has
> and buys that field.

> "Again the kingdom of heaven is like a merchant
> in search of fine pearls who, on finding one pearl
> of great value, went and sold all that he had and
> bought it.

> "Again the kingdom of heaven is like a net which
> was thrown into the sea and gathered fish of
> every sort; when it was filled men drew it ashore

and sat down and sorted the good into vessels but threw away the bad."

A similar collection of ethical sayings is found in Mark 9:37–50. With these the early community could preserve some of the traditions about Jesus and begin to use them in their understanding of the contemporary life of the community. We can also say that the emphasis in the early Church seems to have been not on the cross and resurrection as much as on the eschatological coming of Jesus as Savior and King. Since the Jewish expectation was for a glorious Messiah, the only way they would have accepted a suffering Messiah was if at the same time there was joined the hope that Jesus would return soon and manifest himself not as the one who suffered but as the one who triumphs and who will fulfill the expectations of Israel. Such thoughts caused an emphasis in the early Christology on the theology of exaltation with an emphasis on an imminent parousia.

### Gospel: New Literary Form

What we witness in the early groupings of writings about Jesus is a community of people affected by his life and teachings and desirous of joining the meaning of Jesus, his cross and his resurrection to his teaching message, all for the sake of those who believe and will come to believe. The result of all of this energy is a Gospel, a new literary form.

The word "Gospel" (*euangelion*) is the reward for the transmission of good news, or the good news itself. In the Hebrew of Isaiah 40:9; 52:7; 61:1 the verb *bissar* means to proclaim the good news of salvation. This will influence the New Testament.

The Old Testament tradition as recorded in Second

Isaiah affirms a close link between the messenger of God who proclaimed the eschatological message of the in-breaking of God's royal rule and the message itself.

> The Spirit of the Lord God is upon me because the Lord has anointed me to bring good tidings (*bissar*) to the afflicted (Is. 61:1).

> How beautiful upon the mountains are the feet of him who brings good tidings (Is. 52:7).

The good tidings is the final living word of God that is preached and not a document.

In the New Testament the Gospel is not then a biography of Jesus nor a chronicle of his life and activities but a proclamation of the good news of salvation in Christ.

We can actually examine the four "Gospels" as we have them now and discover that they are joined fragments, each with its own purpose and particular theological approach to Jesus. Born of the faith experience of Jesus by the early Church, each one gives a deeper understanding of the saving presence of God in Jesus. We can even speak of several layers in the Gospels: the foundation which is proclaimed by Jesus himself, the oral tradition that passed from one generation to the next, preserving the meaning of Jesus for new converts, and finally the written traditions that were needed to preserve for all generations the Jesus tradition and which we call the Gospels.

### The Task of Interpretation

All of these layers and divisions, however, do not mean that the early Church was not interested in the facts of Jesus. It clearly proclaimed "how God anointed Jesus of

Nazareth with the Holy Spirit and with power, how he went about doing good and healing all that were oppressed by the devil, for God was with him" (Acts 10:38). The early community of believers, however, was never content to merely recount the facts. If it was good news, then the facts needed to be interpreted so that the meaning was evident to the world. The preachers of the good news were not reporters but prophets: people who heard the word of God in Jesus and who could interpret the religious dimension present or absent in life as a result of hearing that word. Their task was to interpret and tie the meaning to the events much as Moses could act the prophet and give the meaning of the exodus and Mount Sinai experiences to the early Jews.

It is important to realize this interpretive task of the evangelists. None of the Gospels, for example, present an objective account of the multiplication of the loaves. They told the story in a way that the listener could understand the meaning of the event. Compare Mark 6:34–44 with Exodus 16 and Psalm 23 wherein Jesus is the good shepherd who feeds his flock, just as God fed the people with manna in the desert. Compare also John 6:4–14 with the Last Supper narratives in Matthew, Mark and Luke, wherein John presents clear eucharistic overtones to the multiplication of the loaves.

Each Gospel contains both fact and interpretation, both history and theological reflection on the meaning of that history. In the Gospels we see Jesus through the eyes of the faith of the early Church. Surely the disciples had been eyewitnesses of all that Jesus had said and done during his public ministry, but they had often been unable to understand the meaning of the events.

"Who then is this that even the wind and sea obey him?" (Mk. 4:41). But he said to them, "I

have food to eat of which you do not know." So
the disciples said to one another: "Has anyone
brought him food?" (Jn. 4:33).

The disciples understood only after the resurrection when
the Holy Spirit given by Jesus opened up their minds to
understand the meaning of what they had experienced
with Jesus. It is this Easter faith that the Gospel pro-
claims.

Those who preached the good news about Jesus carefully selected the traditions about him that best revealed
the meaning of his mission and the mystery of his person.
The long process of the formation of the Gospel traditions
revealed the effort to unfold the meaning of the facts
about Jesus. This interpretation offered by these early
believers is revealed in the selection of narratives and
sayings. Not everything about Jesus had been included in
the Gospels—"Now Jesus did many other signs in the
presence of his disciples which are not written in this
book" (Jn. 20:30)—but only those things were recorded
which the Church understood to be important for itself
and then for succeeding generations.

### Events Changed in Context

Even the particular form used in the narratives about
Jesus was carefully selected. The wording is chosen to
suggest some deeper meaning such as we have noted in the
multiplication of the loaves. One evangelist will present a
miracle of Jesus and relate the story to the power of Jesus,
while another will take the same event and relate it to the
problems of the early Church. A change in context and
the sequence of events can bring out more clearly the
theological intent of the author. Matthew, for example,
places the stilling of the storm in 8:18 in the context of the
following of Jesus. Three times before he narrates the

event he uses the word "to follow." He arranges the order of events and has a liturgical formula used by the disciples in their fear: "Save us, Lord!" Mark presents the same story in the context of the power of Jesus over evil, and instead of the liturgical formula of Matthew he has: "Teacher, do you not care if we are perishing?" (Mk. 4:38). Since Mark is the source for Matthew, it is evident that context and sequence can alter the meaning.

When the above examples are multiplied it is no wonder that modern scholarship will not accept the Gospels as histories in the sense of contemporary biography. The Gospels are documents of faith coming from a community of faith attempting to proclaim the good news of salvation in Jesus to themselves and to others. This does not mean that there is no history present in the New Testament accounts of Jesus but simply that this history is given specific interpretations.

Since we have spoken so frequently of the proclamation and have noted that the authors selected from a vast amount of material what was to be proclaimed, one might ask just what was the primitive preaching that the early community proclaimed and preserved for us. To discover the answer to this question we turn to the Acts of the Apostles and discover in some of the speeches recorded there what was the proclamation of the early Church.

## The Primitive Kerygma (Preaching)

The speeches of the Acts of the Apostles attributed to Peter (2:14–36; 3:12–26; 4:8–12; 5:29–32; 10:34–43) are compositions by Luke, the author of Acts, and they contain certain Lucan editorial adaptations. It is also the general agreement of scholars that while these sermons were the work of Luke, he did not make them up in their entirety. According to Dodd and others, they contain genuine reminiscences of a very primitive preaching about Jesus.

These memories must go back to the early days of the
Church's reflection upon the events which formed the
formal point of its faith.

The early apostolic preaching, as we have seen, was
the result of the experience of the apostles as well as the
result of the experience of the risen Lord and the gift of
the Spirit. The combination will now form the fundamental unity for the entire New Testament and is discovered
in the accounts in Acts.

### Content of the Preaching

As to the content of the preaching: At the heart of the
Gospel message is the crucified and risen Lord: "You
crucified and killed him by the hands of lawless men. But
God raised him up . . ." (Acts 2:23–24). The same proclamation is found in Acts 3:13–15; 4:10; 5:30; 10:39–40; 13:27–
30.

It is interesting to note the choice of words used to
describe the crime committed by people and the response
of God the Father.

> "do away with" (2:23; 10:39; 13:28)
> "nail up" (2:33)
> "crucify" (2:36; 4:10)
> "kill" (3:15)
> "murder" (5:30)
> "hang up" (5:30; 10:39)
> "God raised him up" (2:32; 3:26; 5:30; 13:33, 37)
> "glorified" (3:13)
> "exalted" (2:32; 5:32)

What the early Church preached was a crucified and
risen Lord. This is the heart of the kerygma and forms an
inner circle that will be surrounded by other aspects of
the meaning of Jesus.

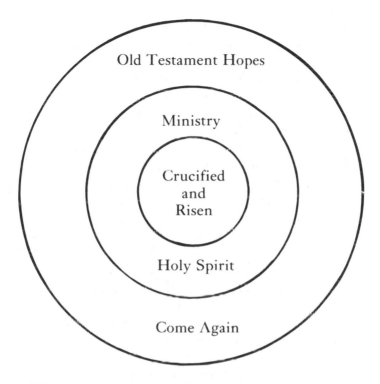

The next element in the primitive preaching is the recollection of the ministry of Jesus: "Jesus of Nazareth, a man attested to you by God with mighty works and wonders and signs which God did through him in your midst . . ." (Acts 2:22). More simply put: "He went about doing good" (Acts 10:38). This forms part of the first outer circle to be completed by the sending of the Spirit by Jesus: "Having received from the Father the promise of the Holy Spirit he has poured out this which you see and hear" (Acts 2:33).

Finally, the second outer circle contains the preaching that Jesus was the fulfillment of Old Testament expectations and he will come again as judge: "He is the one ordained by God to be the judge of the living and the dead" (Acts 10:42).

The purpose of this preaching was to effect a religious experience in the listener, a call to repentance, to change one's way of living, to turn over a new leaf by making an act of faith which was then to be sealed by the acceptance of baptism: "Repent and be baptized, every one of you, in the name of Jesus Christ for the forgiveness of your sins" (Acts 2:38).

From this brief summary of the content of the early preaching, the primitive character of the Church's appreciation of Jesus will be evident. There is no concern about the origin of Jesus, nor of his pre-existence. There is no explicit statement as to the peculiar relationship between God and Jesus as his only divine Son. Nor do we find any explicit statement such as 1 Corinthians 15:3 ("Christ died for our sins") of the redemptive purpose of the death of Jesus. Finally, nowhere is any allusion made to the love of God or of Jesus for people in effecting this good news of salvation. The early preaching was what the followers of Jesus saw as essential for the promulgation of salvation in Jesus.

This is not to imply that the early preachers did not have a profound understanding of Jesus. Rather we must see the preaching as it was and not read back into it what we have learned from later New Testament writings as well as two thousand years of Christian tradition. Perhaps we can better appreciate this preaching if we pay close attention to the titles used in these texts.

### Titles for Jesus: Servant

Jesus is called God's servant (3:13). The apostolic Church very early in its reflection found in the theme of the suffering and glorified servant of God a most congenial vehicle for expressing something of the personal attitude of Jesus. We shall see later how this combination is particularly dear to Mark and his Gospel. It is this glorified servant who suffered and who now is present to the Christian community: "God, having raised up his servant, sent him to you first, to bless you in turning every one of you from your wickedness" (Acts 3:26).

## Messiah

Jesus is also called the Anointed, the Messiah, the Christ. This use in the primitive preaching testifies that in Jesus is found the divinely given answer to the messianic hopes of Israel. "Let the house of Israel therefore know assuredly that God has made him both Lord and Christ" (Acts 2:36; see also 3:18; 10:36). An additional theme, also of importance to the early Church, was the notion that at the second coming the exalted Jesus would enter into his full messianic function: "He may send the Christ appointed for you, Jesus, whom heaven must receive until the time for establishing all that God spoke by the mouth of his holy prophets from of old" (Acts 3:20–21).

## Prophet

The archaic designation of Jesus as prophet in Acts 3:22 probably took its origin from Deuteronomy 18:15 when Moses is reported as predicting the coming of another prophet like himself. This title seems to have fallen from use quickly, with only John 1:45 preserving the title for Jesus, while the other evangelists tended to identify John the Baptist with the prophet of the end times (Mk 9:12–13). Certainly Jesus was a prophet in the Old Testament tradition of one who spoke the word of God and who interpreted the present scene in the light of the presence of God, but for the early Church he was more than just a prophet, which would account for the short-lived use of this designation.

## Lord

One title that seems to imply divinity is that of "Lord." In its Aramaic form (*Mari*) it seems to have been used as an honorific title for Jesus during his ministry. More significant is the liturgical use of the phrase: *Maran atha*, "Come, our Lord," which was probably an eucharistic acclamation expressing faith in the divine character of Jesus (1 Cor. 16:22; Rev. 22:21).

Modern scholars are divided as to whether the title "Lord" actually expressed the Christian belief in the divinity of Jesus, but it should be recalled that the Greek translation of the Old Testament, the Septuagint (LXX), rendered the sacred name *YHWH* as *Kyrios*, Lord. Since the preaching spoke of Jesus as exalted, it could be that his unique relationship to the Father accounted for the evolution of the title "Lord" as a divine title for the exalted Christ.

## Judge

We have noted that Jesus is the judge of the living and dead (Acts 10:42; 17:30–31). In Israel God alone is the judge of the people (Gen. 18:25). Now Jesus in the primitive preaching shares in that prerogative.

## Savior

Finally, Jesus is the Savior (Acts 5:31; 13:23). He it is who will save his people from evil and from the sense of despair that often seems to accompany human life. His saving presence will be felt in the exultant shout: "What shall we do to be saved?" This preaching was directed to outsiders to call them to conversion, but one should also remember that the same testimony is given within the heart of the community when the apostles bear witness to Jesus:

> Now the company of those who believed were of one heart and soul, and no one said any of the things he possessed was his own but they had everything in common. With great power the apostles gave their testimony to the resurrection of the Lord Jesus (Acts 4:32–33).

The community "devoted themselves to the apostles' teaching" (Acts 2:42). Thus, this preaching will be the unity not only of the Gospels but the epistles and of the whole New Testament. Jesus is preached as Lord and Savior. It is his person and his word and his work enshrined in the primitive preaching which unify not only the New Testament but all of Christianity.

When we look at the Gospels we can see that they are the fourfold articulation of the kerygma. Each one has its own genius, born more of the creative dynamism of the Spirit than a mere result of words and deeds. The Gospels are the good news springing from the living witness of Christian faith by four privileged representatives of the apostolic Church. Each author interpreted so as to serve the divine purpose of preaching the saving truth of the word of salvation:

> "Brethren, sons of the family of Abraham, and those among you that fear God, to us has been sent the message of salvation" (Acts 13:26).

### Further Study

C. H. Dodd, *The Apostolic Preaching and Its Development.*

J. Rohde, *Rediscovering the Teachings of the Evangelists.*

# Chapter Two
# The Need for
# a Gospel: Mark

The early preachers of Jesus called for listeners to change their way of living and become part of God's kingdom. From what we can gather from the earliest writings of the New Testament, the letters of Paul, it seems that the earliest followers of Jesus believed in an imminent return of Jesus in glory. When this happened, his reign would be evident visibly and would do away with the then-known political structures. With such a purview the attention was centered not on the past, the beginning of the kingdom in Jesus, but on the immediate future which would break into the present time. Their concern for the present was seen as in preparation for the fullness of the kingdom about to come.

In this context, an elaborative effort to preserve in detail past events would seem unnecessary. If Christ was coming quickly, there was no need to be greatly concerned about the future generations, nor was there a felt need to systematize the life and teaching of Jesus. All this seems evident in a close reading of the earliest writings of the New Testament.

Such a preoccupation with the future, however, does not mean that they were uninterested in the historical Jesus. If Jesus inaugurated the kingdom of God and did so as an itinerant preacher in Palestine, then those who experienced him as the risen Lord through the preaching of the apostles developed a great interest in his teaching as well as in the events associated with his life. It was only natural that anecdotes would be preserved and orally transmitted. People would remember incidents in their experience of the earthly Jesus and tell others. Bultmann's study of the Synoptic tradition shows that sayings of Jesus, his miracles, and his parables circulated throughout the Mediterranean world of Christian missionaries. Specific sayings of the Lord would be used to settle new problems of the early community such as in 1 Corinthians 7:10 ("To the married I give charge, not I but the Lord, that the wife should not separate from her husband") or in 1 Corinthians 9:14 ("In the same way the Lord commanded that those who proclaim the Gospel should get their living by the Gospel"). The problem of apostasy and poorly grounded faith would give rise to the interpretation of the parable of the sower.

### Freedom of the Evangelists

It is not surprising that early in the history of Christianity we should have sayings of Jesus, parables, miracle stories, and collections of quotations concerning him from the Old Testament. What is surprising is the sense of freedom that the authors exercised in using these materials. We have already seen how Matthew and Mark present the stilling of the storm at sea. Theological intent is as important as the particular details. The parable of the sower could become an allegory with such experience of the fallen seed assigned to a group of people actually existing in the early Church. The multiplication of the loaves could be modified to suit the purpose of John as well as Mark. Even Paul who did not know the earthly Jesus felt free to amplify the sayings of the Lord to suit his purpose. How could this be?

It seems that the early Church believed that Jesus himself is God's Word, and so if he was present in his community there was no need to be overly concerned about the exact words of the earthly Jesus. The risen Lord is God's Word and is alive, still guiding the Church. This belief is made explicit in Luke as he recounts the meeting on the road to Emmaus: "And beginning with Moses and all the prophets he interpreted to them in all the Scriptures the things concerning himself" (Lk. 24:27). Jesus continues to teach his Church as the risen Lord.

The same notion is present in John through the presence of the Spirit: "But the counselor, the Holy Spirit, whom the Father will send in my nane, he will teach you all things" (Jn. 14:26). "When the Spirit of truth comes he will guide you into all the truth" (Jn. 16:13). The early Church experienced the presence of the risen Lord, and thus, with the presence of Jesus, what he had done as the earthly master was reshaped to meet the new conditions of the times. Jesus would continue to speak to his followers.

Again, this is also understandable. Remembering isolated events in the life of Jesus or even collecting some of his sayings and using them to respond to the needs of the times makes eminent sense, but to combine these units into a new literary form which we call a Gospel still raises some unanswered questions.

### Why Write a Gospel?

Some crisis, some problem or turning point, some new understanding, had to have occurred which made it imperative to the early Church to gather carefully the traditions about Jesus and combine them into an orderly sequence.

This does not mean that up to this point the Church did without literary activity. The letters of Paul predate the Gospels by anywhere from fifteen to thirty years. It seems that this literary form met the missionary and theological need of the earliest years. Evidently Paul did not think that anything more was needed. Yet, others did see the need for another form of literary activity, and from them we have the four Gospels.

In some sense we can never adequately answer why the Gospels were written. Luke informs us that he wrote his Gospel for Theophilus in order to help him: "It seemed good to me also, having followed all things closely for some time past, to write an orderly account for you, most excellent Theophilus, that you may know the truth concerning the things of which you have been informed" (Lk. 1:3–4). John tells us that he wrote his Gospel so that we may believe: "These are written that you may believe that Jesus is the Christ, the Son of God, and that believing you may have life in his name" (Jn. 20:31).

No doubt these are partial answers, since no Gospel is the work of an isolated individual. If Gospels arose, they met not the need of a literary author but the needs of a Christian community. As each Gospel is different, so the particular needs of the individual communities must have been different.

We also know that as the Church grew, questions would continue to arise. People wanted to know more about Jesus. As the parousia was delayed, a sense of pain was experienced as people awaited the return in glory. A concern for preserving accurately the material about Jesus would have developed especially as those who knew him personally experienced death. Even as they awaited a coming in glory, now delayed, people would have been interested in him when he lived as a man.

Some historical crisis could also have precipitated the writing of a Gospel. We know that there were conflicts between Judaizing Christians and the Gentile converts. Did one have to become a Jew first in order to be a follower of Jesus? A Gospel could help solve some of this tension and begin to move toward a final resolution. A Gospel that could give an opening for a truly Gentile community could give a direction in which the Church could move. For some authors today the crisis between synagogue and Church is evident in the Fourth Gospel and helped the coming into being of that Gospel.

All such crises as well as the natural tendency to preserve traditions were involved in some way in the origin of the Gospels, but, as mentioned above, we cannot grasp the Gospels together without seeing that each one has its own peculiar characteristics. We have to speak not only of the origins of the Gospels but of the origin of the individual Gospel and, in particular, the origin of the Gospel of Mark.

### Mark: The First Gospel

Scholars are not completely in agreement (William Farmer is the leader of the opposing school), but in general we can say that the majority of New Testament scholarship favors the viewpoint that the Gospel of Mark was the first written Gospel, and that Luke and Matthew then used Mark as one of their sources for their own Gospels.

If Mark was the first and if Matthew and Luke used Mark, we can find it helpful to understand Matthew and Luke by examining how they react to Mark. Unfortunately for Mark there is no prior means of comparison. This means that if we hope to understand the meaning of Mark as he arranged the traditions of Jesus, we have to read Mark himself and read him most carefully.

In the past the Gospel of Mark was often thought to be the simplest of the Gospels and the one most closely related to the historical ministry of Jesus without any great theological reflection. More recent work on Mark by Willi Marxsen, Andre Trocme, Howard Kee, and Theodore Weeden, however, shows the Gospel to be like the other efforts to preserve the traditions of Jesus. The Gospel has its own theological perspective and should not be judged to be any more or less historically accurate than the other three Gospels. The days of thinking of Mark as somewhat simplistic with absurd transitions and unresolved conflicts occurring in the Gospel are over. The author is a writer of subtlety with a sophisticated theological mind who faced the problem of ordering a vast amount of material into such an orderly fashion that he actually created a literary form. His genius was recognized by no less authorities than the authors of Matthew and Luke who trust his basic framework and rework their own interpretation of the meaning of Jesus in light of his approach.

To study Mark is not to bypass the depth of John or Paul but to enter into the realm of the insights of scholars as they continue to probe into the origin and meaning of the first of the Gospels with a fresh approach. Mark saw the need to create a Gospel, and if we are to understand that Gospel which he offered us through the early Church, we have to seek to discover the need that Mark himself experienced in the early followers of the Lord.

### History in Mark

On first reading it might seem that Mark constructed his Gospel on the actual historical event of Jesus. Jesus is presented in the Gospel as preaching to the masses of people (chapters 1–8), but when faced with opposition he turns to the small band of followers and speaks only to them (chapters 9–13). He does this because he knows that he must die and that they must eventually be prepared for his passing and to carry on his preaching (chapters 14–16).

Perhaps we could look at the same material and construct the Gospel historically, recognizing that the opposition in Galilee encouraged him to strike at the heart of Judaism in Jerusalem in his effort to help people understand the good news that concluded in Jesus' death.

Such an historical analysis, however, contains many flaws upon closer examination. In reading Mark one might get the impression that Jesus preached in the north, went south to Jerusalem and died, all in one year, with one visit to the holy city. John, however, records many visits to Jerusalem and has at least a three-year public ministry, unlike the one year of Mark. Which Gospel is historically accurate? Some might be tempted to construct an historical account of Jesus by combining the details of all four Gospels. Such was attempted in the nineteenth century, resulting in the conclusion that the Gospels cannot be considered historically accurate accounts of the life of Jesus. The same statement must be true for any individual Gospel. Accurate history is not the concern of Mark.

Paul Achtemeier shows us that Mark also seems to get quite confused when he tries to deal with chronology. In 4:35 we learn that evening had come, but before we have any reference to time again in 6:2, Jesus had crossed the sea, stilled the storm, healed the Gerasene demoniac, made another trip across the sea, healed the woman with a flow of blood, went to the house of Jairus and returned to his own country. Evidently chronology is not important for Mark, nor can we say that geography is his concern. He frequently becomes confused as to location. The Sea of Galilee, for example, is not in the midst of the Decapolis (ten cities).

## Theology, Not History

Needless to say, Mark has arranged his testimony to Jesus not because of history, nor with attention to detail of time and place, but for a purpose that can only be explained through a particular theology. If we can understand the theological purpose of Mark we are well on the way to understanding the Gospel. Such a process, however, is not an easy adventure. We have already noted that

Mark used sources—the collections of sayings, stories, etc., about Jesus. We can actually sift out some of these. This process is known as form criticism. This shows us that the material had circulated long enough orally to be refined and made into a set pattern. Such an effort would in itself involve some theological purpose which would have been different from the theological purpose of Mark. The compilers of these traditions or members of the early Church communities who wished to preserve the sayings or anecdotes of Jesus would have had their reasons, and these reasons would be expressed in the material they collected and arranged. Such material would reflect the level of theological development of the Church in which it first circulated.

### Levels in the Gospel

We have also noted that this material does go back to Jesus himself, which is the first of the three levels found in any Gospel: Jesus, the collected traditions of the community which preserved their understanding of Jesus, and, finally, the Gospels as actually written by the evangelists. To try to reach through the authors of the Gospels and to continue through the early community to grasp something of the historical Jesus is only a limited possibility. We are too far removed in time and circumstances from

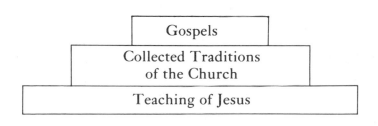

the ministry of Jesus to construct a clearly delineated portrait of the Jesus of history. Thus, we need to be most cautious in making statements about the historical events in the career of Jesus or attestations about the exact words of Jesus. Very often these events and choice of words cannot be disentangled from the other levels of the Gospel.

## The Purpose of Mark

All of this brings us back to the desire to understand the purpose of the Gospel of Mark. Why did he gather the material in existence, and how did he arrange things to suit his purpose, and what was the need in his community to which his Gospel could give a response?

We have previously noted that as early as 1890 Martin Kahler suggested that the Gospel of Mark was a passion story with an extended introduction. This can be accepted as accurate, at least inasmuch as the passion and death of Jesus stands at the center of Marcan theology. This is shown in many ways. A good example is the way in which Mark treats John the Baptist.

The tradition contained in Mark 1:2–8 portrays John as a forerunner of Jesus. Mark also makes him a forerunner of the passion of the Lord. This is the reason for the thematic synchronism in 1:14: the catchword "to be handed over" points to Jesus' being handed over during the passion. The association of the Pharisees and Herodians in 3:6 is to be understood in the same way: there is a relationship between the people who have John executed and those who destroy Jesus.

The mention of the legend concerning the beheading of the Baptist in 6:14–29 between the sending out of the disciples and their return may rest on similar grounds. Mark hardly needs this insertion which disappoints the most elementary chronological expectation in order to fill up the time between the sending out and the return of the disciples as older exegetes supposed. This characteristically Marcan technique of composing by inserting one story in the midst of another connects the Christian mission indirectly with the death of Jesus, to which, according to 1:14 and 3:6, the death of John the Baptist proleptically points. All of these passages conflate the fate of the Baptist with Jesus. This relates the fate of Jesus to his passion at the outset of his ministry and thus illuminates the activity of Jesus from the perspective of the cross. Then the mission of the disciples is joined to the same context of the dying Lord.

### Messianic Secret

Two other Marcan themes can be mentioned briefly. Often Jesus forbids any speaking of who he is. We face what has been called the "messianic secret in Mark." For years, since Wrede first wrote his book on the messianic secret, scholars have tried to study the meaning of this tendency without any complete consensus. Can it be that the need for silence is due to the lack of an understanding of a suffering Messiah?

### Disciples' Misunderstanding

A second Marcan theme is the apparent lack of understanding of Jesus on the part of the disciples. Can we say the same thing with regard to the followers of Jesus: that their lack of understanding was their failure to see the meaning of the suffering and death of their Lord?

To return to the purpose of this chapter: To understand the meaning of the Gospel of Mark demands a clear appreciation of how he ordered the traditions about Jesus to suit the needs of his community. It seems that the key to understanding Mark is to know the meaning of the death of Jesus. It is in this perspective that he writes, and it is within this perspective that we have to read the final product.

No doubt there was a need for a Gospel. Mark chose to write an orderly account of the meaning of Jesus by concentrating on his cross and death. As we study the passion in Mark we will receive further insights into the community for which he wrote that will in turn add to our awareness of his purpose in writing.

### Further Study

W. Kelber, *The Kingdom in Mark.*
W. Marxsen, *Mark the Evangelist.*
P. Achtemeier, *Mark.*

# Chapter Three
# The Passion

Since the advent of biblical criticism scholars have studied the Synoptic Gospels to discover the teachings and deeds of Jesus, the way in which the early Church transmitted and altered these traditions, and the theological concerns of the individual evangelists. Although the passion narratives form the climax of the Gospels and occupy about fifteen percent of the tradition, the research had been directed more to the pre-passion parts of the Gospels. Several reasons account for this tendency to overlook the passion account. It was often thought that this material was the most traditional and most historical, and this offered the least amount of research on its use. Also, since it was so closely related to the historical Jesus, there would be little influence coming from the early Church and even less from the individual evangelists.

In contrast to the earlier stages of study, the last decade has witnessed an explosion in studies on the passion accounts. Each passion narrative is seen as much a result of theological reflections as any other part of the Gospels. This is especially true for Mark, for in the passion narrative we not only have the climax of the Gospel, but the climax of the theology of Mark. The recent collection of articles on the passion edited by Kelber gives an excellent survey of the material.

We have already noted that, for Mark, Jesus is himself the model for discipleship. Just as Jesus has given up, and as has John, so will the disciples. They see in him the obedient and righteous Son of Man who suffers. To understand the meaning of the passion, it is important to

study the predictions of the passion in chapters 8:22—
10:52.

## Cures of Blind Men

Surrounding this section, which is the central section
of the Gospel, Mark places the healing of the blind men in
8:22–26 and 10:46–52. Throughout the Gospel, Mark seems
to wish to give a catalogue of all of Jesus' cures. Out of the
nine stories of healing, only one illness is shown occurring
more than one time: that is the case of blindness, and these
miracles surround the central section of the Gospel. It
cannot be by accident that the author chooses to situate his
teaching on the meaning of the death of Jesus. When
someone discovers the significance of the passion of the
Lord, that person "sees" and his blindness is removed.

Throughout the Gospel Jesus attempts to give sight to
his disciples. He tries to teach them the meaning of his
impending passion and death. Continually he fails to pen-
etrate their understanding. The Jesus who could give sight
to the physically blind could not give sight and understanding to his disciples. For Mark, this is one of the great
tragic motifs of the Gospel. As he tells his story, he is
constantly reaching out beyond the disciples to his own
listeners, attempting to help them to understand what the
disciples had so significantly failed to understand.

Mark accomplishes this by three blocks of carefully
constructed prediction units.

## Predictions of the Passion

And he began to teach them that the Son of Man
must suffer many things and be rejected by the
elders and the chief priests and be killed, and
after three days rise again (8:31).

For he was teaching his disciples, saying to them, "The Son of Man will be delivered into the hands of men and they will kill him; and when he is killed, after three days he will rise" (9:31).

"Behold, we are going up to Jerusalem; and the Son of Man will be delivered to the chief priests and the scribes and they will condemn him to death, and deliver him to the Gentiles; and they will mock him and spit upon him and scourge him and kill him; and after three days he will rise" (10:33–34).

### Misunderstanding of the Disciples

And he said this plainly. And Peter took him aside and began to rebuke him, but turning and seeing his disciples he rebuked Peter and said, "Get behind me, Satan. For you are not on the side of God, but of men" (8:32–33).

But they did not understand the saying and they were afraid to ask him (9:32).

And James and John, the sons of Zebedee, came forward and said to him: "Teacher, we want you to do for us whatever we ask of you." And he said to them, "What do you want me to do for you?" And they said to him, "Grant us to sit one at your right hand and one at your left in your glory." But Jesus said to them, "You do not know what you are asking. Are you able to drink the cup that I drink or to be baptized with the baptism with which I am baptized?" And they said to him, "We are able." And Jesus said to them, "The cup that I

drink you will drink, and the baptism with which
I am baptized you will be baptized, but to sit at
my right hand or at my left is not mine to grant,
but it is for those for whom it has been prepared"
(10:35–41).

### Teaching by Jesus to Correct Misunderstanding

And he called to him the multitude with his
disciples and said to them, "If any man would
come after me, let him deny himself and take up
his cross and follow me. For whoever would save
his life for my sake will lose it; and whoever loses
his life for my sake and the Gospel's will save it.
For what does it profit a man to gain the whole
world and forfeit his life? For what can a man
give in return for his life? For whoever is
ashamed of me and of my words in this adulterous and sinful generation, of him will the Son of
Man be ashamed, when he comes in the glory of
his Father with the holy angels" (8:34—9:1).

And they came to Capernaum, and when he was
in the house he asked them, "What were you
discussing on the way?" But they were silent for
on the way they had discussed with one another
who was the greatest. And he sat down and called
the Twelve; and he said to them, "If anyone
would be first he must be last of all and servant of
all." And he took a child and put him in the midst
of them, and taking him in his arms he said to
them, "Whoever receives one such child in my
name receives me; and whoever receives me receives not me but him who sent me" (9:33–37).

And Jesus called them and said to them, "You
know that those who are supposed to rule over
the Gentiles lord it over them and their great
men exercise authority over them. But it shall not
be so among you; but whoever would be great
among you must be your servant, and whoever
would be first among you must be slave of all.
For the Son of Man also came not to be served
but to serve and to give his life as a ransom for
many" (10:42–45).

### The One Who Serves

This final section closes with the climactic interpretation of the meaning of Jesus: He has come to serve and to
give his life. No wonder there is misunderstanding on the
part of the disciples. They are concerned with the Jesus of
glory who will establish his kingdom and offer them a
share.

Jesus teaches them that not only is the way of self-
giving and suffering that of the Son of Man, but it is also
the way of his followers. As one studies these three predictions two things become evident: the variety in the references to the passion and the lack of variety in the
references to the resurrection.

The references to the passion vary between the two
distinctive ways of speaking of the passion of Jesus in the
New Testament. The first uses the Greek word *dei* (must)
which is often used to designate divine necessity, especially the divine necessity revealed in Scripture ("Why do the
scribes say that first Elijah *must* come?"—Mk. 9:11;
"Brethren, the Scripture *had to be* fulfilled"—Acts 1:16).
The second and third references use the word *paradidomai*
(to deliver up) which is a technical term in the New
Testament to describe the passion of Jesus (For I received

from the Lord what I also delivered to you, that the Lord Jesus on the night he was *delivered* up . . . —1 Cor. 11:23). We have already seen that the same word is used in reference to John the Baptist (1:14), and it is used in Mark in connection with the potential fate of Christian martyrs in 13:9 ("For they will deliver you up to councils"). All are delivered up—John, Jesus, and the disciples; each suffers a passion. One prediction speaks of divine necessity; the others speak of the passion common to all followers of the one true God.

### Comparisons of the Predictions

The variations in the predictions go beyond the use of the above words. The first and third offer considerable details concerning the passion itself, with the third almost a summary of the events in chapters 14–15. The second prediction is more terse to the point of bluntness. Such variations tend to highlight the stereotyped nature of the reference to the resurrection: ". . . and after three days rise again . . . after three days he will rise . . . after three days he will rise." Clearly, as Perrin shows in his study of the resurrection, Mark is not nearly so interested in the details of the resurrection as he is in those of the passion. This does not mean that he is uninterested in the resurrection but that the passion is emphasized to suit his theological purpose.

If this is the central section of the Gospel a more careful analysis of the other material contained in this section will be helpful to us in our effort to enter into the meaning of the witness of Mark.

### Discipleship

Between the second and third blocks of material, Mark has inserted a teaching section that has to do with what it really means to be a disciple. Single-mindedness, divorce, acceptance of children and riches are discussed. The section ends with a pericope of hope and expectation of the age to come:

> Peter began to say to him, "Lo, we have left everything and followed you." Jesus said, "Truly I say to you, there is no one who has left house or brothers or sisters or mother or father or children or lands for my sake and for the Gospel who will not receive a hundredfold now in this time, houses and brothers and sisters and mothers and children and lands, with persecutions and in the age to come eternal life. But many that are first will be last and the last first" (10:28–31).

### Transfiguration

The story of the transfiguration in this section (9:2–8) also functions as a message of hope and is symbolic of the post-resurrection situation. Since Moses and Elijah were thought to be in heaven, when Jesus is transfigured while speaking with Moses and Elijah, he is being seen proleptically in the post-resurrection state and situation. He is in heaven with God and the ancient prophets, awaiting the moment of his return to earth as the powerful and glorified Son of Man.

The disciples within the story of the transfiguration are urged to obey the words of Jesus, and in this context the content of those words concerns the true meaning of discipleship. The reference to Elijah in verse 13—"But I tell you that Elijah has come and they did to him whatever they pleased, as it is written of him"—shows that his way in life was also a way of suffering parallel to that of the Son of Man and the disciples. It seems that Jesus is specifically referring to John the Baptist which, as we have seen,

Mark identifies with the fate of Jesus. The healing of the boy after the transfiguration could have some reference to the resurrection. The boy is described as looking like a corpse so that the crowd judged him to be dead. When Jesus healed him, Mark may have been symbolizing that Jesus will enable others to rise from the dead and to be with God just as he will rise and is with God. The only condition is that of faith. Since Mark uses the healing of the blind men for symbolic purposes, he may be attempting the same thing in this pericope.

### *Anthropology, Not Christology*

It is important to note that the motif and movement of the entire section is not so much on Christology (although that is part of the meaning) but on anthropology: Mark wishes to speak about true discipleship. Jesus is the suffering Son of Man and he is the model for all disciples. Mark is not concerned solely about the death of Jesus but his mode of living as well. The author wishes to present his way of suffering and his rejection, and finally, in 10:45, the climax of his thinking concerns the servanthood of Jesus. Mark is concerned about the cross, but not the cross as making atonement for sins as much as the theology of the cross that involves suffering in obedience. It is God's decision that his Son must suffer and so the Son willingly accepts his fate. It must be, for so God wills it. Jesus is patterned after the righteous sufferer in Psalm 22:

> My God, my God, why hast thou forsaken me?. . .
> Yet thou art holy, enthroned on the praises of
>      Israel. . . .
> Yet thou art he who took me from the womb,
> thou didst keep me upon my mother's breast.
> Be not far from me, for trouble is near
> and there is none to help (Ps. 22:1, 3, 9, 11).

Since Jesus is the model for others in his living and in his dying, in his death we see the deepest meaning of the cross in Mark's theology. The death of Jesus lays open a quality of life which is the pattern and example of what true life is for all men. The true follower of Christ must take up his cross daily and follow the Lord; there is no optional road, no substitute and no other means by which a person can be a disciple. No wonder the offer is only to the brave of heart. To find life is to live as Jesus did, which involves a share in his sufferings. That is how the true believer will walk. "For whoever is ashamed of me and of my word in this evil and adulterous generation, of him will the Son of Man be ashamed when he comes in the glory of the Father with the holy angels" (8:38—9:1). To be ashamed of him is to reject his suffering. "My words" is the expectation on the part of Jesus that his disciples will follow him even if this entails the road to suffering. As a result Mark brings his Christology into the closest contact with the Church and believer and in so doing reveals the incarnational Christology of power and depth that will pervade his Gospel. Mark presents in his Gospel an apocalyptic drama in which he and his community are self-consciously caught up in events they view as the end of history. The Gospel portrays this drama in three acts.

### Delivered Up

First John preaches and is delivered up (1:14). Then Jesus preaches and he is delivered up (9:31; 10:33; 14:41). Finally the Christian preaches and is delivered up (13:9–13) with the hope directed toward the return of Jesus as the glorious Son of Man: "And then they will see the Son of Man coming in clouds in great power and glory" (13:26); ". . . and you will see the Son of Man sitting at the right hand of power, and coming with the clouds of heaven" (14:62). For Mark the cross and suffering are always in

John ----------→ Preaches ------→ Delivered up

Jesus ----------→ Preaches -------→ Delivered up

Disciple -------→ Preaches ------→ Delivered up

the foreground but in the background as the foundation for hope is the resurrection. The glorified Lord will bring his faithful followers to share in that same glory.

### Further Study

M. Kahler, *The So-Called Historical Jesus and the Historic Biblical Christ.*
W. Kelber, *The Passion in Mark.*
N. Perrin, *The Resurrection according to Matthew, Mark and Luke .*
T. Weeden, *Mark: Traditions in Conflict.*

# Chapter Four
# The Son of Man

We have already seen that a principal aim of the Gospel of Mark is his Christology which carries with it an anthropology. The understanding of Jesus implies equally an understanding of what it means to be human. The religious dimension of human life is presented by the evangelist through the mouth of Jesus. The author leads the reader into a deeper understanding of Jesus himself as well as an appreciation of what it means to be a disciple.

## A False Christology

Theodore Weeden holds that Mark's set purpose in emphasizing the Christology of one who suffers before he is to enter into glory is to counteract an appreciation of the glorious Christ without the willingness to accept the suffering, obedient Christ. A false Christology of glory had affected some of the community, and thus Mark had to correct this inadequate view of the Christian life with his insistence on the suffering Son of Man. We shall return to this point later. For the present it is enough to be aware that Mark is careful to teach about the suffering Messiah before he is to enter into his glory.

In spite of the classical work by Hans Tödt, *The Son of Man in the Synoptic Tradition*, there is no scholarly consensus concerning the precise meaning and importance of the title in pre-Christian tradition. It certainly was important for Mark, and it would be helpful for us if we had some appreciation of the origin of the title and the meaning of the title in Judaism.

The phrase can mean simply "man" in a generic sense as found in Psalm 8:4:

What is man that thou are mindful of him,
of the Son of Man that thou dost care for him?

This also may have been the meaning in the pre-Marcan tradition in the use in Mark 2:28:

So the Son of Man is Lord even of the Sabbath.

The original meaning may have been that every man is able to make decisions with regard to the rightful observance of the sabbath, since the sabbath was made for man and not vice versa. The use of "man" and "Son of Man" stand in parallelism. The original meaning of the story of the disciples going through the fields of standing grain may have been an effort on the part of Jesus to give "man" simply as a human being authority over the sabbath. There is no doubt, however, that in Mark this meaning is overlaid with the thought that Jesus is the Son of Man and is the actual Lord of the sabbath.

### Old Testament Meaning

The Old Testament usage can be found in Daniel 7:13 in which the title is used to describe the heavenly figure in the fifth vision of Daniel. The basic meaning here is that the figure stands for the faithful remnant of Israel.

The title is also found in the apocryphal book 1 Enoch (chapters 46–53) and carries with it the theme of judgment. In this usage the Son of Man is also called the anointed one and the elect one, thus joining the image of the Son of Man to the eschatological figure of the Messiah of Israel.

With these varied uses, joined with that found in Ezekiel, it is difficult to draw any definite conclusions as to the precise meaning of the title in Judaism. What is clear, however, is that by the time of Mark the title had been firmly attached to Jesus even if Jesus himself never actually used the phrase.

### Son of Man in Mark

Norman Perrin has devoted much study to the meaning of the Son of Man in Mark. His conclusions in general are warmly accepted. We can note with Perrin that Jesus himself is the only one who used the title, and he did so always in the presence of his disciples or the inner circle of Peter, James and John. Certainly we can question whether Jesus ever used the title himself and associated it with dying and rising, since it is found only in the Marcan tradition and not in the other Synoptics. The use of the title in the Gospel of John carries another nuance with the theme of suffering eliminated.

### Two Levels of Meaning

In the use by Jesus two levels or phases can be distinguished. Five occurrences derive from traditional material at Mark's disposal and appear to have been left untouched by the evangelist:

> ... and how it is written of the Son of Man that he should suffer many things and be treated with contempt (9:12).

> And then they will see the Son of Man coming in great power and glory (13:26).

> For the Son of Man goes as it is written of him, but woe to that man by whom the Son of Man is betrayed (14:21).

> The hour has come; the Son of Man is betrayed
> into the hands of sinners (14:41).

> And you will see the Son of Man sitting at the
> right hand of power and coming with the clouds
> of heaven (14:62).

Since these references seem to have been left untouched
by Mark, they must have been consistent with the peculiar
Marcan emphasis in their original form, but they tell us
little about the originality of Marcan use.

Throughout the Gospel the title refers to Jesus as the
one who was betrayed (14:21) and arrested (14:41), suffered
(9:12), died (10:45), was raised from the dead (9:9), and was
seated at God's right hand in heaven (14:62).

In Mark, each prediction of the passion is followed by
misunderstanding and a teaching about disciplehood. This
central section of the Gospel constitutes Mark's concept of
discipleship and culminates in 10:45 with the theme of the
servant for all. This treatment is also the climax of the
treatment by Mark of the Son of Man.

There is a clear progression in the use peculiar to
Mark from an understanding of earthly authority of the
Son of Man to the necessity of the suffering of the Son of
Man and finally to the apocalyptic authority and the final
dramatization of the soteriological significance of the passion. All of the these themes are united by Mark in his
choice of title Son of Man.

### Son of Man—Son of God

There is a clear pattern in the creative use of the title
Son of Man in the Gospel of Mark. He juxtaposed the title
with the more significant title Son of God to give a cor-
rected understanding of belief in Jesus. He will join the

earthly authority of Jesus as the Son of Man to Jesus as the Son of God. In 3:11 a Marcan summary emphasizes that Jesus exercises his authority on earth as Son of God, while we have seen that in 2:10 and 2:28 the emphasis is on Jesus and his authority as Son of Man. In 8:38 the tone is that of the apocalyptic authority of the Son of Man which is carefully linked by a time reference seven verses later to the voice of the transfiguration that addresses Jesus as "my beloved Son." The high priest asks Jesus if he is the Son of the Blessed, and the reply is in terms of the Son of Man (14:61–62). For Mark the meaning of Son of God is related to the meaning of the Son of Man.

Mark will unite the various themes of suffering, apocalyptic authority and soteriological significance by using the title Son of Man in each case. The title was used before him in reference to the earthly ministry of Jesus. To this Mark joined the emphasis on "power." We have noted the use of the title in the apocalyptic literature in the Old Testament. Mark could take that title and adapt it easily to his own perspective. The title was also used in connection with the passion. Mark developed the passion predictions and the teaching about discipleship. Finally, the saying about service became soteriological in the affirmation that Jesus as Son of Man came to serve others.

### Threefold Purpose in Mark

There seems to be, according to Perrin, a threefold purpose in the Marcan use of Son of Man. First, Mark counteracted an emphasis on the glorious Christ by including the notion of suffering Son of Man. Second, this suffering is also part of the ministry and experience of the disciples. Finally, this suffering was actually the way to the experience of the saving presence of God for Jesus and will be the same for all of his followers. All of these are bound together in the title Son of Man.

*Further Study*

N. Perrin, *A Modern Pilgrim in New Testament Christology.*

H. Tödt, *The Son of Man in the Synoptic Tradition.*

# Chapter Five
# The Power of Jesus
# in Word and Miracle

For the author of the Gospel of Mark the preaching and teaching of Jesus were fundamental to the whole meaning of Jesus as well as his power to work miracles. We have noted that the heart of the Gospel is the suffering Son of Man, but it is also the activity of the Son of Man that must be understood if we are to enter into the fuller meaning of the good news according to Mark.

### Preacher and Teacher

Paul Achtemeier would divide the activities of Jesus as preacher and teacher mainly because Mark included in his vocabulary both words and seems to have a slightly different appreciation with each activity as verbally expressed in preaching and teaching. Rather than complicate the issue unduly, we will treat both activities under the notion of the power of Jesus in word.

It is also true that the Son of Man performs miracles, since, more than is true of any of the other Gospels, Mark fills his account of Jesus with references to his miracles. In fact, if we were to compare the four Gospels there is a decline of interest in the miraculous activity of Jesus as we progress from Mark to Matthew to Luke and finally to John. For Mark, Jesus was one who performed acts of power as part of his ministry. He was powerful not only in word but in miraculous deed.

When we begin to read the Gospel one of the first things we read is that Jesus preached (1:14–15): "The Gospel of God is at hand." This opening chapter ends with a sense of compulsion that Jesus experiences to go about the land preaching (1:38).

### *Little Interest in Content*

We should note that Mark does not dwell on the actual content of the preaching of Jesus. Even when Jesus sent out his disciples to preach, there is no mention of what precisely they were to preach (6:12). There is only mention of repentance which is the same that we heard in the preaching of Jesus in 1:15 and the very content of the preaching of John the Baptist in 1:4.

The apparent lack of interest in the actual content of the preaching can be explained by the way Mark identified Jesus with the kingdom of God. For Mark, Jesus is the beginning of God's final and glorious rule. It is not just what Jesus said that was important but also how he lived and that he died, as well as what he actually did. All is part of the Gospel and thus all is part of the preaching and all is involved with the in-breaking of the reign of God.

Mark also speaks about preaching in 13:10 and 14:9:

And the Gospel must first be preached to all nations (13:10).

Wherever the Gospel is preached in the world, what she has done will be told in memory of her (14:9).

With these passages we have seen all of the references in the Gospel that deal with preaching. There are, however, other activities which deal with the same reality, although the word "preaching" is not used.

To "speak the word" can be seen as a parallel to preaching (1:15, 45; cf. 14:9), and it can also be seen as a parallel to teaching (4:33; 8:32; cf. 9:31). Evidently Mark was not overly careful or greatly concerned with his particular choice of vocabulary. Jesus was the presence of the reign of God, and he himself was the Gospel. For this reason he could interchange vocabulary, since all of the words and ideas would help fill out the fuller meaning of Jesus. One such choice of vocabulary that seems to have had great import to the author of the Second Gospel, however, is the word "teaching" and "teacher."

### Teacher

Jesus often seems to function as a teacher of the law, a "rabbi." In 10:17 a man asks Jesus about eternal life, and Jesus reacts out of the tradition of the law just as a rabbi or scribe might do.

People, whether friend or foe, also address Jesus as a teacher (12:14, 19, 32; 9:38; 10:35; 13:1). He taught in the synagogue, beside the sea or wherever crowds had gathered. Also, Jesus seems to identify his activity as teaching:

"Day by day I was with you in the temple teaching" (14:49).

He also used the title "teacher" when he instructed his disciples to prepare the Passover:

The teacher says: "Where is my guest room, where I am to eat the Passover with my disciples?" (14:14).

Mark saw teaching as a regular activity of Jesus, and when the disciples return they narrate not only what they have done but what they have taught (6:30), even though they were not instructed to teach (6:7, 12–13). For Mark, if Jesus taught, then his disciples had to teach just as his

Church would teach. The combination of the teaching activity of Jesus and of the Church is clearly seen in the parables. Mark saw the parables as a principal way in which Jesus taught, and then the Church could use the parables in its own teaching.

## The Parables

Modern scholars such as Joachim Jeremias see the parables as the most characteristic element in the teaching of Jesus as recorded in the Gospels. They have the stamp of a highly individualistic mind and carry a strong ring of authenticity. But while most agree on the close connection between Jesus and the parables, there is no great agreement on the interpretation of the parables. The word parable (Hebrew: *mashal*) means a simple comparison or a similitude: the eye is like the light of the body (Lk. 11:34). But when these simple comparisons become elaborated into stories, we have parables proper, a peculiar figure of speech which carries power in its very use of words. Even when scholars such as Norman Perrin, Dan Via, Robert Funk and John Dominic Crossan become involved in the careful study of the parables as literary teaching devices, we should not lose sight of the original sense of comparison. Parables are not carefully constructed allegories in which every detail has some hidden meaning. The situation presented in the story is what is used to present the lesson, with no great interest in trying to discover symbolic elements in every aspect of the story.

## Symbolic Elements

This is not to say that in some parables some of the characters should not be identified. In the parable of the prodigal son the father is clearly God, the young man is a sinner and ultimately the Gentiles, and the older brother represents the righteous who practices obligation piety (the Jews). But the parable is the situation that is constituted by the interplay of the characters: the love of God is freely directed to all who seek it. The main point of the story could be lost if we become too involved with allegorical interpretations.

We have noted that parables were the chief teaching device of Jesus and that Mark saw that the Church must continue the teaching function of the Lord. As a result many of the parables were embellished by the early Church as it sought new meaning in the teachings of Jesus and as it tried to apply the parables to the present situation of the followers of Jesus.

If we are to understand the teaching of Jesus and of the Church, we have to follow the concern of Jeremias and try to reconstruct the life-situation in which the parables were first used by Jesus and the situation of the apostolic Church within which the parable tradition took its final form.

## Reinterpretation of the Parables

Previously we noted that the Church was not so much concerned with the actual words of Jesus as it was concerned with his prolonged presence as teacher in the community. The Church would never merely hand on what Jesus had actually said to a particular group when he first uttered the parables, for it would be more interested in what the parable might mean today.

The most obvious reason for this reinterpretation of the parables was the change in audience. It would seem that very few of the parables were originally addressed to the circle of disciples but rather to those outside (Mk. 4:11), to the multitude of people gathered to listen to Jesus, or even to his opponents.

The parable of the laborers in the vineyard (Mt. 20:1–

16) was originally addressed to those Pharisees who criticized the good news of Jesus. The Lord attempted to show them through a parable how unjustified and loveless and unmerciful was their opposition. In the Gospel of Matthew, we see how the audience has changed and how the same parable is addressed to the followers of Jesus who have to be willing to allow all people into the kingdom and rejoice that many share in the same good fortune. A study of the parable of the sower will make these points more evident.

### Parable of the Sower

The parable of the sower is a good example of a combination of the teachings of Jesus and that of the early Church. It is the opinion of most contemporary scholars that Mark 4:13–20 represents a homiletic commentary on the parable as expressed by Jesus by the early Church. Scholars reached this conclusion because verses 13–20, in contrast to the actual parable, are un-Hebraic in style and contain a whole series of words which appear nowhere else in the sayings of Jesus, but which are very characteristic of the later epistles in the New Testament. These verses then are a result of the Church's efforts to draw the meaning from the parable and apply it to the situation of the times of the community. Thus it is easy to miss the precise meaning of the parable as intended by Jesus and to concentrate instead on the meaning as taught by the early Church. This is not to say that one is preferred to the other. Rather, both situations, that of the ministry of Jesus and that of the Church, give us a fuller appreciation of the parable.

In light of the further development of parable studies by Perrin, Via, Crossan, etc., we can also say that it is possible to prescind from both situations and allow the parable as metaphor to affect us in understanding the teaching of Jesus even as it is overlaid by the experience of the early Church. What is evident is that the parables as the principal means of teaching by Jesus give opportunities for all of his followers to increase their self-understanding as believers

### The Meaning of the Parable

To return to the parable of the sower, it is clear that the main point in the teaching of Jesus is the wonderful power of the seed to bring forth a marvelous harvest, no matter what the obstacles.

When a person sows a lawn, he is not concerned if some seed falls on the driveway, or some falls into the flower beds, or some falls on the road, or some falls on the edge of the property, to be lost forever as far as growth. He knows that with care there will be a lawn.

In spite of the problems and failings in his ministry, Jesus knew that in him God the Father had made a marvelous beginning and in the end there would be a great harvest, there would be a lawn, there would be the kingdom of God on earth.

The harvest had been a traditional image to describe the final fulfillment. It is used in the Old Testament to describe the fruitfulness of the messianic times (Am. 9:13–15). It is found also in the psalms:

May those who sow in tears
    reap with shouts of joy.
He that goes forth weeping,
    bearing the seed for sowing,
Shall come home with shouts of joy,
    bringing his sheaves with him (Ps. 126:5–6).

To human eyes the preaching and labors of the whole line of prophets culminating in the ministry of Jesus must have seemed in large measure a failure, but Jesus knew otherwise. In the parables he teaches that in spite of indifference, opposition and unwillingness to understand, the seed which Jesus had implanted in people would bear fruit. There would be a glorious harvest.

In the original formulation of the parable there was little or no interest in the specific nature of the obstacles to the reception of the seed. The beaten path, the birds, the stony ground, and the thorns are simply typical obstacles taken from the experience of farming. The point is that no obstacle can hinder the power of the word of God. This is the main meaning of the parable, and it continues to have meaning to the Church in every age. The scandal, however, of the apparent failure of the power of God's word remains. The marvelous seed of new life, the word of God, will always experience obstacles, but where it is received the results are a transformation and a fruitfulness in love which is the sign of God's activity in the world, and in the end it will be powerfully effective. No obstacle, or power, or force can imprison the word of the Lord.

## Application by the Church

In the apostolic Church, however, the preachers chose to bring out an aspect of the parable which had been only secondary. What precisely were the obstacles which sometimes prevented the fulfillment of God's saving plan with regard to particular individuals? The question which the preacher addressed to the listeners in recounting the parable was: "Are you perhaps one of those who, for whatever reasons, refuse to accept the word of God?" In this perspective it was easy for the preacher to find in the agricultural obstacles a counterpart to the potential problems in the lives of his listeners. The situation of the community of Mark which witnessed some who belonged

only for a time gave the preacher the opportunity to tie
the situation of the Church to the actual words in the
ministry of Jesus.

This allegorical interpretation, found in Mark 4:13–
20, which was used to bring out the present obstacles in
the Church, is surely heavy and ponderous but it does not
destroy the parable. Such a development continues the
teaching of Jesus in the actual Church of the apostles by
applying the parable to the situation in which the early
believers found themselves. Mark 4:13–20 bears witness to
the Church's fidelity in attempting to draw all the meaning possible from the teaching of Jesus and make it fully
relevant to the Church's contemporary situation.

### Miracle Worker

Another example of how the author of the Second
Gospel preserved traditions about Jesus and added to them
is his account of Jesus as a miracle worker.

The ancient world was filled with magicians and
wonder workers. Both Jews and Greeks had their share of
those people associated with marvelous deeds. Rabbis
healed the sick, conquered evil spirits and even made ugly
women beautiful. The Greek world had its magicians and
devotees of gods who made the lame walk and the blind
see. That Jesus was a miracle worker does not set him
apart from many of his contemporaries. A contemporary
New Testament scholar, Morton Smith, even presents
Jesus as a magician. To perform a miracle does not in itself
attest to the identity of the presence of God's envoy or
that the miracle worker was the one who would inaugurate the kingdom of God. Even the miracles themselves as
performed by Jesus are open to various interpretations.
We can read the miracles of Jesus from our own perspective, and they appear to be signs of the presence of God

with him. To his opponents, however, they were proof that he must be destroyed because he was involved with the power of evil:

> "He is possessed by Beelzebul, and by the prince of demons he casts out demons" (Mk. 3:22).

Even his family thought he was mad after they witnessed his deeds of power:

> And when his own heard it, they went out to seize him for they said, "He is mad" (Mk. 3:21).

With such a mixed background it is a marvel that the miracle stories survived in the early tradition. In fact, the tack of some of the Fathers of the Church was to concentrate on what Jesus taught and avoid the ambiguity of the miraculous.

But for Mark, this was not the solution. Evidently Jesus did perform miracles, and if they could be ambiguous, Mark decided to preserve the stories and give them his own interpretation or at least the interpretation of his community.

### Structure of the Miracles

The miracles themselves have a distinctive structure. First the problem is stated, then a solution is given, and finally some proof is attested to show that the solution did in fact solve the problem. Further details can be added to the stories, but the structure remains virtually unchanged. When we encounter a theological interpretation, we can strip off the added elements and always come back to the basic structure. This is particularly true in the Gospel of John wherein the interpretation occupies more attention than the miracle itself.

*Theological Interpretation*

Mark joined his theological interpretation by actually adding additional meaning to the miracle through his inclusion of other material or by giving the story a new framework that would alter its meaning. The healing of the paralytic is a good example of the insertion of theological issues.

The problem is stated in 2:2–4: friends brought the paralytic but they could not reach Jesus.

The solution is found in verses 4–5 and 11: they take off the tiles from the roof, and Jesus tells him to take up his pallet and walk.

The proof is found in verse 12: the paralytic rose and walked and all marveled.

In the midst of this story occurs the theological discussion on the power of Jesus to forgive sins. Notice how verses 5a and 10 repeat: "He said to the paralytic . . ." This is a clear sign of an interruption. It is also clear that the theological issue is more important than the miracle for us as well as for the community of Mark.

The Jews always associated sin with physical illness. This gave Mark the possibility for his theological interpretation. The man is obviously worthy of being cured, as is evident in the care and concern shown by his friends. Notice that the man himself says nothing, but Jesus forgives him his sins. The Church of Mark as well as of today needs the forgiving presence of Jesus even though his physical presence can no longer heal us of our physical infirmities. Mark carefully situated his theological meaning to enhance the miracle of Jesus in his ministry and thus gave to his community a sense of the continuing presence of Jesus to forgive sins. We can recall the miracle of the ministry of Jesus but grow in understanding of his presence to his community as one who heals them of their sins.

*The Fig Tree*

A minor miracle story that has always caused confusion to readers of the Gospel is the destruction of the fig tree in 11:12–35. This is joined to another account which also causes problems for readers: the cleansing of the temple. For Achtemeier the combination of these miracles is a Marcan literary characteristic.

The first story seems to place Jesus in a bad light since he seems to take out his frustrations on a fruit tree that was not bearing fruit, even though it is clearly stated that it was not the season for figs (11:13). Why curse a tree for not bearing fruit out of season?

*Cleansing of the Temple*

The story of the cleansing of the temple also seems out of character. Jesus was not the type to become so angered. In many circumstances he faced evil but always dealt with the problem in a gentle way.

To us it may seem out of character, but for Mark the story deals with more than the anger of Jesus at some activities within the temple precincts. By his action Jesus demonstrated that the practices necessary for the normal functioning of the temple had ended. If there were no animals for sacrifice, there could be no sacrifice. If no shekels were available, the support of the temple and priesthood must end. If no vessels could be carried through the temple, then all activity relating to cultic celebration must cease. The temple cleansing represents Jesus' prophetic and symbolic act of ending temple worship. To this Mark has joined the destruction of the fig tree. The fate of the fig tree will be the fate of the temple. Both will be destroyed. Mark has preserved the story of the fig tree and placed it in the context of the cleansing of the temple to tie a theological interpretation to both incidents.

Previously we have seen how Mark and Matthew preserved the miracle of the calming of the storm on the lake and how each gave it a theological interpretation to suit his own purpose. We could examine the miracle stories in all four Gospels and draw similar conclusions. Each evangelist was concerned with preserving these authentic traditions of Jesus but would do so in his own way with his own purpose in view.

With regard to Mark it is evident that he continued the process of adapting and interpreting miracle stories as he had adapted and interpreted the teaching of Jesus to suit the needs of the early Church. Both were sharpened to show that Jesus was powerful in word and in miracle in his public ministry but was still present in the Church as equally powerful in word and deed for those who, through their faith in him, joined themselves into a fellowship of people whose Lord he would always remain. The power of Jesus is still present in his Church, which alone would be sufficient reason for Mark to write a Gospel.

### Further Study

P. Achtemeier, *Mark.*
J. Jeremias, *The Parables of Jesus.*
N. Perrin, *Jesus and the Language of the Kingdom.*

# Chapter Six
## The Disciples Before
## the Word of the Lord

A frequent comment when dealing with the disciples in Mark is that as the Gospel unfolds the followers of Jesus seem to grow not in understanding but in misunderstanding. The Twelve appear as ignorant, ambitious, insensitive and, in general, failures. In the other Gospels they do not fare so poorly, since Matthew and Luke seem to modify the extreme position found in Mark.

One might ask if such a picture painted by Mark can be historically accurate. The response to that question is two-sided. Certainly the disciples were failures, since they did not follow the Lord to the cross, but they could not have been complete failures, since out of their faith came the Easter faith that was the source of the Jesus tradition. Secondly, as we mentioned previously, the picture painted by Mark seems to be a deliberate extreme. Could this be due to the set purpose of his Gospel?

### Theios Aner

Theodore Weeden holds that the disciples symbolize the heresy of those who held that Christ was a *theios aner* (a divine man), a miracle worker, and were overly concerned with the theology of glory rather than that of the cross of the Lord. This view, however, seems in itself to be an extreme, since it is hard to imagine that Mark would portray those closest to Jesus as representatives of a heterodox Christology. Nevertheless, it should be admitted that Mark does present an unusual portrait of the disciples, and there must be some explanation.

While we have stated that there is a tendency to portray the disciples in a less than favorable light, a careful reading of the Gospel shows that this is not always the case. In some instances Mark is more sensitive and positive with regard to the closest followers of Jesus. This is seen in the calling of the disciples in 1:16–20. Jesus calls, and they immediately follow him. The same attitude is present in 10:28 in which Jesus assures them that since they have left all to follow him, they will receive a reward here as well as in the afterlife.

### Followers and the Twelve

It also should be recalled that there is a distinction between the followers of Jesus and the Twelve. There were women who followed Jesus and remained faithful to the end. In 14:50 all of the closest followers flee from the garden, while in 15:40–57 the faithful women follow Jesus to the cross and prepare him for burial. These same women seem to be the first to learn of the empty tomb and are called to proclaim the resurrection to the Twelve. Thus it is not accurate to speak of all of the followers of Jesus in the same way or to see them in the same light all of the time. Evidently Mark was careful in his portrayal of the followers of Jesus, and we must pay attention to his proper perspective.

Previously we noted the relationship between Christology and anthropology in Mark. Perhaps the clue to understanding the role of the disciple in Mark, like that of the Gospel of John, is to see the disciple in relationship to the Christology of Mark. The suffering Son of Man expects his disciples to live a life that will also lead to suffering. The disciples, then, in the Gospel account of

Mark will have two roles to play: they are important for the public ministry of Jesus and they will mirror the problems that anyone who chooses to be a follower of Christ will experience. This will be more evident if we examine the material on discipleship as contained in chapters 8–10.

We have already seen that in these chapters we have the three predictions of the passion (8:31; 9:30–32; 10:33–34). We have also seen that Mark always joins a saying about discipleship to those predictions of the passion, making it quite explicit that a similar fate awaits those who follow a suffering leader. Even when he spoke of the reward of discipleship he includes the phrase "with persecutions" (10:29–30), making it clear that the follower can expect a similar fate as the master. As the glory of the resurrection was preceded by the cross, so the path that leads to the kingdom of God will be strewn with pain and suffering. Jesus is the one who will give his life for others (10:45), and thus the disciple must follow along the same path.

Also, in this section we have the account of the transfiguration. During this religious moment the Father tells the chosen disciples to "listen to him" (9:7b). As Jesus moves from the mountain of the transfiguration back through Galilee (9:30–58) and on toward Jerusalem (10:1–45), Mark through a series of detached sayings and dialogues presents the meaning of discipleship and the necessity of renunciation. These are the words which Jesus speaks following the divine injunction to the disciples: "Listen to him."

### Following the Lord

The disciples must take up their cross and follow him (8:34), renounce all honors and ambitions and seek to be the servant of all (9:35), sell all and give to the poor (10:21), and, finally, give up their very self (8:35). The disciple must risk all in an act of loving confidence in the God who had given them Jesus and who had raised Jesus from the dead.

Because Jesus followed the road of humility and suffering in service, emptying himself (Phil. 2:7–8), the disciple is one who is called to make himself least among his brethren:

> "Whoever would be first among you must be the slave of all" (Mk. 10:44).

The lowly people, the little ones, are the models and the signs of the presence of Jesus, for it is to the child, those who are unassuming and dependent on God, that the kingdom belongs:

> "Let the children come to me; do not hinder them, for to such belongs the kingdom of God" (Mk. 10:14).

In spite of all these clear teachings throughout this section the Twelve still seem to be blind and narrow-minded, seeking status and power for themselves in the future kingdom of God. Their experience on the mountain left them confused. Why such talk about suffering and death concerning God's chosen one? Was not Elijah to come first and restore all things and usher in a reign of glory? Jesus answered that Elijah had indeed come, but the restoration did not mean an end to suffering for Elijah himself (John the Baptist), nor for the Son of Man, and thus not for the disciples of the Son of Man (9:19–13).

## Disciples as Servants

In 9:31–37, as they proceed to Jerusalem and the cross, the followers continue to be preoccupied with petty matters such as procedure in the kingdom of God. In this context Jesus speaks: "If anyone wishes to be first he must be least of all and the servant of all" (9:35). Mark joins this to the saying of Jesus concerning receiving a "child in his name" (9:36–37). Rather than seek honor and riches and power the disciple must seek to make himself the least of all if he hopes to be part of the kingdom of God.

In the story of the man casting out demons in the name of Jesus who was not one of the followers of Jesus (9:38–41) the same idea is present. The disciples must do away with petty jealousy and their own prerogatives and recognize that they do not have an exclusive claim over the saving presence of God. If someone is doing good in the name of Jesus, then he is part of the entourage even if he has not been identified or approved by the Twelve.

### Authority

Mark 10:35–45 contains some of the most important texts on the nature of discipleship and brings this section to a close. It also contains the classical text on the nature of authority in the Church.

The text begins by placing the Twelve in a most unfavorable light. They are guilty of the fault of self-seeking and jealousy. When the sons of Zebedee seek a place of preference in the kingdom, the rest of the Twelve become indignant with the two brothers. Jesus replies by stating that they are not to exercise authority over the brethren in the same way that secular rulers exercise control. They should not "lord it over," should not act like the "high and mighty," but they are to model themselves after Jesus and how he exercised his authority. The Lord of all had striven to be servant of all. His followers could do nothing less.

Of all the disciples the one who seems to stand out the

most in Mark is Peter. For this reason some have thought
of Mark as a disciple of Peter. Peter is called first (1:16), his
name is the first that is changed (3:11), and his name
appears first in the list of disciples. Peter is the first of the
inner circle (5:37; 9:2; 13:3; 14:33) and he functions as a
spokesman for the group (1:36; 8:29; 9:5–6; 10:28; 11:21).
His denial is foretold explicitly (14:29–31) and it is later
narrated in detail (14:66–72). Peter is also named when the
women are told to tell the disciples about the resurrection
(16:7), and he seems to have remained with Jesus the
longest during his passion, with his own repentance for
his sin attested (14:72).

### Peter

If we were to examine these passages in detail it
would seem that Peter is presented in both a favorable
light and an unfavorable light. Mark expresses the best of
being a disciple: "You are the Christ" (8:29) and the worst:
"And Peter took him aside and began to rebuke him. . . .
'Get behind me, Satan' " (8:32–33). The first one called,
Peter is also the one who repeatedly denies the Lord even
after he has professed to be faithful to the end. He is the
faithful and the unfaithful lover, the one who understood
and the dullest of heart. Such a portrayal does not neces-
sarily mean that Mark wants to denigrate Peter and then
rehabilitate him and place him in a position of authority.
Rather the successes of Peter and his failures are the
successes and failures of the Twelve and, we might add, of
all the followers of the Lord. If the disciples in Mark
depict the kinds of problems any follower of Jesus is likely
to experience in the course of following the Master, then
Peter shows us that the career of a single disciple knows
the heights of faith as well as the dregs of despair. The
disciple must drink of the heady wine of enthusiasm and

commitment as well as the sobering water of personal failure. The disciple has the experience of Tabor as well as the pits of the Gehenna of rejection, denial and despair.

### Suffering

There is no doubt that discipleship is important in the Gospel of Mark, but as we have seen there is no understanding of discipleship without knowing the meaning of Jesus. Mark understood Jesus as the suffering Son of Man. This is the key to his Christology as well as the key to understanding the meaning of discipleship. The fate of Jesus is ever present throughout the Gospel and seems to hang over the entire account of the ministry of Jesus like a pall. From the beginning the Master experiences opposition and misunderstanding, and the climax of the Gospel is his sad and cruel death. From beginning to end the Jesus of Mark's Gospel is the suffering Son of Man, and unless that fact is clearly understood there is no meaning to Jesus.

If the disciples fail to understand during the public ministry, it is because to understand Jesus is to see him as the one who suffered and died. Only in the light of the cross can the life of Jesus be illuminated. The disciples could not know the real Jesus until he had suffered and died. Their failure to understand during the ministry is grounded in the Christology that permeates the account of Mark. The use of the word "permeates" is deliberate, for this is a sad Gospel of pain and suffering.

The inability of the Twelve to understand is not dependent on their own psychology. During the ministry they had yet to see Jesus suffer and die; they had yet to come to grips with their own sharing in this suffering; they were too concerned about the wonders of the kingdom without seeing the price that would be paid to inaugurate the reign of God. When they saw him suffer and die, then they could understand him and begin to understand their own calling and destiny. Jesus "had to suffer" (8:31), as it was written of him (8:14–21), and thus there existed no possibility of even understanding the meaning of Jesus until he had died his death on the cross.

Mark saw value in presenting Jesus as powerful in word and miracle, but this is not where one finds the meaning of the Lord. We may be encouraged to follow him because of his power, but we will become his disciples in truth only when we have accepted him as one who suffered. Just as the disciples could not understand him apart from his final destiny, the same is true for believers of all times. Perhaps this is part of what Mark has to say to succeeding generations of believers: to know Jesus and to love him and to follow him is to willingly embrace the folly of his cross.

### Further Study

P. Achtemeier, *Mark*.
T. Weeden, *Mark: Traditions in Conflict*.

## Chapter Seven
## Faith and the
## Community in Mark

The Gospel of Mark, as should be evident at this point, is not an account of historical fact but a testimony of faith. He expresses his understanding of faith not in theological statements but in narrative forms. In the events of ministry, in the course of action, in details of time and place, and not just in the spoken word are found the hidden expressions of faith. What people actually say in Mark is commented upon in the course of action in which they are involved.

### Faith

The faith of Peter is seen in the testimony that Jesus is the Christ in 8:29, and also in the various actions that portray his relationship to the Lord. There is no explicit expressed faith on the part of the paralytic nor of his companions in chapter 2, but their actions give evidence of its presence. The individual becomes a believer when he repents and accepts the Gospel and then in faith is joined to the community that shares that faith. We have already treated many aspects of faith throughout these pages, but the final element in the understanding of faith in the Gospel of Mark involves the role in the community. An individual who has contributed much in this aspect of Marcan theology is Howard Kee, and to him the writer is much indebted.

## *Community*

The grouping of people in Mark is a voluntary association of individuals who have actually listened to the preaching of the good news and have changed their way of living as a result of their commitment to Jesus. This very fact involves them in a relationship with other believers.

The corporate nature of faith is seen in the meaning of the reign of God (1:14). For Mark this is a future reality:

> "There are some standing here who will not taste death until they see the kingdom of God come with power" (9:1).

However, it is also a reality that has drawn near:

> "The kingdom of God is at hand; repent and believe in the Gospel" (Mk. 1:15).

It is characterized by growth and by conflict, and it must be entered and received (4:26–30; 3:24; 9:44; 10:23–25; 12:34; 3:8). The conflict is seen in the demonic forces that seem to erupt frequently in the Gospel. Jesus explains to his own that by his presence the destruction of the rule of Satan is accomplished. The exorcisms of Jesus actually bind Satan and presage his demise.

## *Kingdom as Gift*

The notion of receiving and entering is Mark's way of showing that no one can merit the kingdom but must receive it as a gift. However, there must still be personal involvement and the actual reception. God freely offers but the individual must also freely accept. This reception is not only for the future, but for the present as well.

People enter the kingdom, having accepted it as a gift,
now.

A key to understanding the entrance into the kingdom is expressed in the story of the man who sees the
commandments summed up in the law of love. He is
described as "not far from the kingdom" (12:34), and thus
very close to entering into it. At the same time the one who
enters must acknowledge the demands. All worldly security
is abandoned and all riches are given over to the poor.

The community that results from the joining together
of those who have entered the kingdom involves a present
age of discipline and renunciation in which a new type of
community living is accomplished with a promise of an
eternal communal life with God and with other believers.

### Community as Family

Mark offers another image of the community: that of
family. In Mark 3:31–35 the real family of Jesus are those
who do the will of God. This family does not hold to
bonds of blood or to sexual distinction. Anyone who believes, who does the will of God, forms part of the family
of Jesus and all are on an equal footing. This new family
implies a split with the old family, seen in the actual
experience of Jesus. Jesus' mother and brothers come to
take him away (3:31). Mark also states that this actually
took place at his home (3:19). Jesus makes the break from
the former bond in a family to create a new bond of faith.
As Jesus himself had to set the pattern for being part of a
new group, so his followers must do likewise.

### Future Rewards

The rewards of this new life are set out in exaggerat-
ed form in chapter 10: one hundred times as many homes
and brothers and sisters and children and lands. This is to

show that the acceptance of Jesus in faith does not imply a deprivation but actually brings about a fellowship superior to anything that had preceded it. The reward is completed with the view to the future age which will be nothing more than eternal life.

Mark continues his theme of a community of faith when he presents Jesus as the shepherd to his flock of believers. He uses the image twice: 6:34 and 14:27. In each case the interrelationship between leader and group is made explicit.

The later reference occurs on the night before the crucifixion. The shepherd will be struck and the sheep will be scattered. But Mark will not leave his listeners disheartened. Jesus will be raised up and gather them together in Galilee (14:28).

The reference in the sixth chapter demonstrates the compassion of Jesus for the crowds who are like sheep without a shepherd. Jesus must respond to their needs and so he teaches them (6:34). His concern continues when they are hungry, and so he feeds them (6:35–44). As once God called his people out of Egypt and cared for them in the desert, so Jesus will sustain his people until they enter the promised land of fulfillment. He will not forget them but will care for them as a shepherd cares for his sheep.

### Covenant People

A final image under which Mark presents his community of faith is that of a covenant people. It is mentioned directly only once in the Last Supper scene:

"This is my blood of the new covenant which is poured out for many" (Mk. 14:24).

The reference to the blood of Jesus refers presumably to the sacrifice of Jesus which will ratify the covenant and accomplish a new relationship with his people: "which is poured out for many." In the following verse the ultimate outcome of this new covenant is the consummation of the kingdom of God:

> "I shall not drink again of the fruit of the vine until that day when I drink it new in the kingdom of God" (Mk. 14:25).

The prophet Jeremiah presents the classical presentation on the new covenant in chapter 31. He emphasizes two components: forgiveness and the worldwide scope of the covenant community. Both features are present in the Gospel of Mark.

We have already seen how Mark joins the notion of forgiveness to the power of Jesus in the cure of the paralytic in chapter 2. We have also noted that the cursing of the fig tree (11:12–14) is an allegory on the destruction of faithless Israel. The lesson to be drawn, however, is less a polemic against Israel as a warning to the new covenant people (11:20–25) which culminates in an appeal to exercise forgiveness toward one's fellow human being:

> "And when you stand praying, forgive, if you have anything against anyone, so that your Father who is in heaven may forgive you your trespasses" (Mk. 11:25).

As for the all-encompassing nature of this covenant community, we read in Mark that the angels will "gather his elect from the four winds, from the ends of the earth to the ends of the heavens" (Mk. 13:27).

Even more telling is the reference in Isaiah that speaks of the coming gathering by God:

> Everyone . . . who holds fast my covenant, these I will bring to my holy mountain and make them

joyful in my house ... for my house shall be
called a house of prayer for all peoples. Thus says
the Lord God, who gathers the outcasts of Israel.
I will gather yet others to him besides those
already gathered (Is. 56:6–8).

Mark quotes the central portion of this quotation in the
story of the cleansing of the temple (11:17) as he demonstrates that the old limitations on the access to God are
over. Now there is free access to all people. Those of
Jewish background. The only criteria for entrance are
those of faith, the hearing of the word of God and the
repentance that will change a person's life. The result is a
community of people who trust in the Lord and live a
shared life of faith together as they await the final outcome and the consummation of the reign of God.

### Further Study

H. Kee, *Community of the New Age: Studies in
Mark's Gospel.*

A. Trocme, *The Formation of the Gospel According
to Mark.*

*Chapter Eight*
# The Origin of Mark

Most works on a Gospel will begin by responding to some of the curious questions associated with the origin of that Gospel: Who actually wrote the Gospel? Where was it written? When was it written? These questions are of particular interest today, since by now many people have heard that the names we associate with the Gospels may not be the names of the actual authors. I have chosen to wait until this point to deal with some of these curious questions with the hope that a study of the Gospel will be of some assistance in understanding the tentative nature of my response to the above questions.

## *The Author*

The Gospel itself never states anything about its author, its origin or the time of composition. For us to respond to these questions we will have to deal with inference within the Gospel as well as conjecture and seek some evidence in other historical works. At the end we may still be no closer to any conclusive answers than we are at the outset, but at least we will have tried to respond to some questions that often pique the curious.

Evidently in the early years of the Church there was no great interest in the authors of the Gospels. As we have already noted, the communities were more aware of the continual abiding presence of the Lord with them and thus need not have been concerned with his actual words.

This same conviction would have allayed any fears about the authenticity of the Gospel accounts. But when Gospels began to multiply and a greater time distance developed between the historical Jesus and the Church, many became concerned about the reliability of the Gospels. If many were in existence, how can one judge those that were in close continuity with Jesus and his disciples? One such criterion could be the author. If there was a way to establish the reliability of an author, then this would guarantee his Gospel. If we could ascribe the Gospels to apostles or those associated with apostles, then this would give greater credence to the Jesus tradition as expressed.

### Anonymous Evangelists

With regard to the question as to who wrote the Gospel of Mark, first we should recall that nowhere does the author identify himself. The same is true for all of the Gospels. Matthew does not identify himself, nor does Luke; in the Gospel of John the author seems to identify himself with the beloved disciple, but this cannot be equated with the apostle John (21:24).

In the past we have assumed that the authors were male, but this too is an unfounded assumption. Both in Luke and Mark women figure rather prominently and in general seem to be more faithful followers of the Lord. Could this imply that the author of Mark or Luke was a woman? All we can say is that the gender of the author also is uncertain. Obviously the author saw no need to identify himself or herself, and the early Church was content to deal with anonymity. We have seen that the Gospel was composed of available traditions about Jesus which the different evangelists arranged to their own purpose. If these traditions were generally known to the communities, there would be no great concern about preserving the identity of the one person or persons who arranged the material to suit the peculiar needs of the community. We have noted that the work of the editing gave a peculiar stamp to the material, but it was not a question of composing new material.

### Efforts to Discover the Identity

Some people will turn to unusual details in the Gospel and seek the identity of its author—for example, some will say that the only reason that the fleeing of the naked young man in 14:51–52 was preserved was due to the fact that the young man was the author of the Gospel. Such conclusions seem ill-founded.

The earliest reference we have to the author of the Second Gospel is found in the writings of Eusebius, bishop of Caesarea in the fourth century. This author attempted to write a history of the Church from its inception and used as one of his sources the writings of an earlier historian from the second century called Papias.

Papias claimed to have known some of the apostles and thus would have been a third-generation believer. He deals with the origins of the Gospels and claims that from Aristion and John the Elder he had learned that the author of the Second Gospel was Mark, who had been Peter's interpreter. The traditions then would be coming from Peter. Eusebius makes his own commentary on the matter by emphasizing that Mark was not a follower of the Lord but merely tried to preserve the recollections of Peter without trying to make an arrangement of them. It is this tradition that lies at the foundation of our ascribing the authorship of this Gospel to Mark, the companion of Peter. From the same author we learn of the origin of the Gospel of Matthew, an apostle who wrote first in Aramaic, and the origin of the Fourth Gospel as the account of John the apostle. We also learn that Luke was the traveling companion of Paul, and so his Gospel becomes reliable because of his association with Paul.

In the various books of the New Testament we find reference to people named Mark. On the assumption that only one Mark was prominent in the early Church, all of these references are seen to be related to the author of the Second Gospel.

John Mark was a companion of Paul and Barnabas on missionary journeys and then disagreed with Paul so that he would have nothing to do with him (Acts 12:12; 13:13; 15:37–40). He in turn is identified with the Mark mentioned in Philemon 24 as the fellow worker of Paul. Mark is again mentioned in Colossians 4:10 and in 2 Timothy 4:11 and 1 Peter 5:13. With so many references to Mark in the New Testament we can easily flesh out something of the identity of the author of the Gospel. The only flaw in the construct is the assumption that there could be only one Mark who was among the early converts to Christianity. As a fact, we know that Mark was one of the most common and popular names in the Roman empire. Who is to say that each reference to Mark referred to the same person? Would it not be more likely that it referred to different persons?

We do, however, end up with the name Mark. If the concern was with authenticity would it not have been smarter to ascribe the Gospel to Peter instead of his companion? It may well be that the author of the Second Gospel was named Mark, but that is about all we can say about him. We do have the reference in Eusebius, but from other studies we are aware of the tentative nature of the historical accuracy of this early historian, and he in turn relied on another historian who is not always the most accurate.

## Conclusion

Our conclusion as to the author of the Gospel of Mark is tentative and unsatisfying. Perhaps it is unnecessary to ask the question. We have an account of the Jesus traditions that the early Church accepted as reflecting the authentic faith of the community. Who wrote it is not as important as its contents. If the Gospel can express faith and can aid faith, then it matters little as to the actual identity of its author. As documents of faith, the Gospels transcend a need for authenticity of authorship.

## Geographical Origin

With regard to its geographical origin, we have even less to guide us. Eusebius says nothing. The early traditions that associated Mark with Peter placed Mark in Rome at the time of the death of Peter, and thus the origin of the Gospel was Rome. This also would seem to be in accord with the general tone of the Gospel which seems to be more Gentile-oriented than Jewish-oriented. In the cryptic greeting from "Babylon" sent by the author of 1 Peter to "my son Mark" (1 Pet. 5:13), if Babylon is interpreted as Rome, then some will find further evidence for Rome as the origin of the Gospel. This also presupposes that Peter is the author of 1 Peter, which is more than questionable. Some find further evidence for a Roman origin in the use of Latinisms in the Gospel. Such, however, is not a clear argument, since mixed cultures often borrowed words from various languages, just as English is filled with French words.

The question of suffering in the Gospel has helped people to associate the Gospel with the persecution of Christians under Nero. We know from ancient historians that Nero laid the blame on the burning of Rome on

Christians and that they were actually persecuted not far beyond the confines of Rome. If the community was persecuted and persecution was associated with Rome, then this would give some evidence to the origin of the Gospel in Rome. To counteract this argument we also know that Christians were persecuted by Jews.

Other possible places of origin for the Gospel are Palestine or Syria. Since the author associates chapter 13 with the destruction of the temple in A.D. 70, some would argue that the Gospel came from a region affected by the events of 66–70 and the Roman conquest. The problem with this hypothesis is that the author seems to presume that his readers do not understand Aramaic, the common language of Palestine, since he translates all Aramaic phrases into Greek and he is greatly confused as to Palestinian geography, as we have previously mentioned.

These days more and more scholars are locating the origins of all of the Gospels in Syria or Asia Minor. We know that this area was the strongest mixture of Jewish and Gentile Christians and would have early developed a need for the Gospel, but to group all of the Gospels in the same geographical area does not deal sufficiently with the circumstantial origin of the Gospels.

### Conclusion

As with the case of authorship, so with the question of origin we remain in the dark. Tradition has associated Mark's Gospel with Rome, and that has as much foundation as any other possible place. Once again we may be asking the wrong question. It matters little exactly where the Gospel had its origin, provided that we recognize some of the circumstances in the Gospel as depicting environmental conditions rather than try to discover the environment and then use the environment to explain the

Gospel. The former approach is essential for a fuller understanding of the Gospel; the latter is dangerous, since it is founded on such weak evidence.

## Date of Composition

We finally come to the question of date. In some senses we have more evidence here than in the two previous questions, but once again cannot avoid the shadows.

Since the majority of scholars believe that Matthew and Luke used Mark as a source, as we have previously noted, then Mark has to pre-date these two Gospels. Since we have evidence in Matthew and Luke for a developed Church, we can set limits for the earliest point in time in which they could have been written. Also, since we can conclude from these Gospels that the temple has already been destroyed, we have additional information as to the *terminus a quo* of Matthew and Luke. They could not have been written before the year 70.

We also have learned from our study that the Gospel of Mark presupposed the existence of material that circulated in separate units. We would have to allow enough time for the traditions of Jesus to develop into literary units, as well as enough time for the question of the parousia to be discussed. Most scholars will place the origin of Mark in the decade between 60–70. Some might be happy with this conclusion, since it is the most definite answer yet made as to the origin of the Gospel. While this is the general conclusion of scholars, that does not mean that it is without its problems. While we can find reason for stating that Matthew and Luke were written after the destruction of Jerusalem, there are counter-reasons as well. We can feel secure that Mark 13 refers to the conditions during the Jewish war of 66–70 before the actual outcome with the destruction of the temple, but the same conditions would have been present when Herod the Great waged war in Palestine seeking to impose his rule on the Jews in A.D. 37, and even to jump into another century the same conditions would have prevailed in A.D. 135 when Hadrian destroyed the city of Jerusalem. There is no intent to suppose that Mark was written in the second century by including this war but rather just to demonstrate how the same facts can fit different circumstances.

### The Unknown

We are forced to conclude with as much darkness as when we began. Repeatedly I have stated that the early Church was concerned with the presence of Jesus in its midst. It was not overly concerned with his actual historical words, and it seemed to freely develop and alter historical circumstances. If it was so little concerned with these important aspects of the historical Jesus, we should not be surprised if it was not concerned with the time, place and authors of the Gospels. Provided that the Gospels were an authentic expression of the faith of the Church, they were accepted as used as a means of bolstering that faith. With the passage of time there developed a concern for authenticity as the early community receded into the background of history and new believers were asked to carry on the Jesus tradition. At this period we have the birth of concern for authorship.

For the Church today we have accepted the Gospels as documents of faith; they have proven over two thousand years that they express and bolster faith. If their authors chose anonymity, they are part of that great throng of believers who have preceded us in faith and whose contribution was the passing on of the Jesus tradition from one generation to another. As we have been blessed with their expression of faith, we can recall their memory, whoever they were, and hold them in benediction.

### Further Study

P. Achtemeier, *Mark.*
A. Jones, *The Gospel According to Mark.*

# Chapter Nine
## The Meaning of Mark

Biblical scholars can often be accused of dealing with esoteric knowledge divorced from the reality of the Christian life or at least so far separated from the ordinary life of believers that it seems unrelated to faith. A study of the Gospel of Mark, as is true for a study of any book in the New Testament, must make the bridge from the text to the life of the believer. If the Bible is in truth the word of God and if the word of God is alive and effective, then there must be means by which knowledge can be turned to the service of faith.

In the first chapter of this book we stated that old documents do not easily speak to the contemporary mind even if those old documents are taken from the Bible. To understand how we can move beyond the expression of faith in the New Testament to discover the ever-present reality demands people who read and think and sometimes pray.

### The Sad Jesus

Mark gives believers the opportunity to think after they have read, and this can be a catalyst that prompts prayer. His Gospel is not a very happy one, but often life is not very happy. Jesus is sad. He comes to offer a sense of liberation and freedom, but he experiences only shackled people who seem to be content in their misery. He thinks that people will change their hearts, but he gradually realizes that a change in heart is too much to ask for on their own. Only when he has lived his life and experienced the pain and suffering of every man as the Son of Man can some people turn from their sense of pain and seek resurrection in faith. There is a glory that is associated with Jesus, but not without the cost of human suffering, just as in every truly valuable experience in life some price is paid.

## Suffering Today

To someone who lives in the final quarter of the twentieth century, pain and suffering are real. Perhaps they are no more real than at any other moment in history, but after all we have to live in this period and no other, and thus the pain and suffering need no comparison. It might be easy to settle into the sadness and allow the pain to engulf a person, but the Gospel of Mark says no. There is pain that is all too real, but there is also glory and even anticipated glory.

The passion of Jesus hangs over his ministry like a veil as more and more people reject him, but at the same time there are those who "do the will of God" (3:35) and become his mother and brothers and sisters. The resurrection is predicted as well as the passion (8:31; 9:31; 10:34). There is no pain that is beyond the influence of goodness and the Spirit of Jesus. If Jesus could experience the suffering of the Son of Man, know rejection and misunderstanding even on the part of his closest friends, and still believe in a resurrection, and promise the same to his followers, then all people of all times can take comfort in the suffering Son of Man who lived and died and rose in glory. Life is sad; the Gospel of Mark is sad. Life has its moments of glory; the Gospel of Mark has its glory.

## Hopeful Vision

Living in isolation has never brought much comfort. Joining with others who share a common vision makes the vision more clear and gives courage to the pursuit.

Jesus offered people a vision. It is a better thing to bless than to curse, to forgive than to refuse the offer of peace. Love is the better alternative and makes a person close to the kingdom of God. To enter into such a vision demands a support as well as an invitation. Jesus challenged his followers to join him, but only after he made it evident that he loved them.

A rich young man came to seek this vision. Jesus looked upon him and loved him and then challenged him (10:21). Jesus promised him a share with himself and his followers. He would not be alone as he sought the vision of eternal life, but first he would have to make his commitment in faith. No one could be forced, but the invitation had to be freely accepted as it was freely offered. The young man walked away sad. He sought the vision, but could not accept the demands.

To his own, Jesus turned and reminded them what price a person has to pay in pursuing a vision. The cost is steep, but the company is grand. With hyperbole Jesus claims to grant hundreds of brothers and sisters and friends and homes if only his listeners will cast their lot with him.

## Cost of Discipleship

Faith is not throwing something away or losing what a person has, but perfecting what is already there. Faith does not isolate but joins people together in a common goal with a common means to attain that goal: the good news of Jesus.

Mark will not forget the cost but will teach clearly the gains and promise a sense of belonging. Jesus will be the shepherd who cares for his flock; Jesus will be the guide who continues to teach and unravel the mystery of the meaning of life. All a person has to do is to turn in faith, to repent and believe the good news.

As a believer Mark gives guidance by preserving the teachings of Jesus and adapting them to his own Church. The parables of Jesus have a powerful effect on listeners, since they give assurance of a future as well as instruction for the present. There will be a marvelous harvest because God has so decreed. Already the growth is taking place in spite of all obstacles. No one can inprison the word of the Lord. No power, no force, no person, no regime, no law, can prohibit the growth that God has so ordained. "Let him who has ears to hear me, hear" (Mk. 4:9).

## Evil

Miracles happen. The ship of Peter may experience troubled waters, and there are dark forces of evil that can surround the community, but no believer should lose faith. Jesus may appear to be sleeping, but calm will be restored by the presence of the Lord.

Demons can inflict individuals as well as groups. Whole institutions can be infected with evil forces, but the reign of God has begun in Jesus. He has bound up Satan, and now evil is making its final assault, knowing that its reign has come to an end.

Again, for people in the last quarter of the twentieth century it is surely not so evident that evil is bound. Mark deals with the reality of evil all around him and remains convinced that Jesus and his power for goodness will ultimately bring victory.

The disciples in Mark are often failures. They are

ambitious and lack understanding. They are insensitive to the needs of Jesus, with their leader and spokesman, Peter, the epitome of the best and the worst. He is smart enough to recognize the presence of God in Jesus but too blinded to know its meaning. He believes but often fails in that belief and needs assurance and acceptance. He recognizes his sins and weeps (14:72) and eventually becomes the rock for his fellow believers.

### Faith: A Continual Acceptance

Faith is not a once-and-for-all acceptance of the Lord. Faith is a daily effort to perdure in a commitment in spite of failure and sin. There are no plastic saints in the Gospel of Mark, only people who struggle between the whole-hearted commitment that comes only in death and the selfish opportuneness that keeps Christianity as insurance. The believer knows the failure of despair, the tragedy of sin, even as the follower of the Lord delights in his enticing presence.

For the contemporary believer who is tempted to see Christianity as leisure activity, Mark recognizes the failures and reminds those who listen that faith can live with sin provided that Christianity is living in the heart and not on the sleeve.

The Gospel of Mark, like any Gospel, remains so many printed words unless someone opens its pages and reads and thinks and prays. If scholarship can help in the thinking, then it can be a surer foundation for the prayer. Christians need to have their faith nourished, for they are surrounded by forces at least indifferent to the Gospel if not hostile. Mark will not give answers but rather will unfold the responses that already exist in the human heart. If there is sadness it will be turned to joy, for the "time is fulfilled, and the kingdom of God is at hand; repent and believe in the Gospel (2:15) of Jesus Christ, the Son of God" (1:1).

### Further Study

S. Blanch, *The Christian Militant: Lent with St. Mark's Gospel.*

# Selected Bibliography

Achtemeier, Paul J. *Mark: Proclamation Commentaries* (Philadelphia: Fortress, 1975).

One of the more significant attempts to update readers in Marcan studies. The author deals with Mark from a scientific viewpoint but in clear readable style.

Barclay, William, *The Gospel of Mark* (Philadelphia: Westminster, 1956).

This work by the well-known British scholar is dated but still offers valuable insights for the general reader of Mark. It is especially suited to preachers.

Best, Ernest, *The Temptation and the Passion: The Markan Soteriology* (Cambridge: University Press, 1965).

A careful analysis of the place of the devil in the Gospel and the struggle between the power of evil and Jesus that presents the teaching of Jesus directed to the cross. The cross is judgment borne by Jesus for the sake of others. The author relates the cross to the resurrection which then creates the new community.

Blanch, Stuart, *The Christian Militant: Lent with St. Mark's Gospel* (London: SPCK, 1978).

A popular meditation on the entire Gospel divided for each day of Lent. The author, bishop of York, sees the Gospel as ideal for the Christian militant engaged in conflict with the powers of evil.

Burkill, Thomas, *New Light on the Earliest Gospel* (Ithaca: Cornell University Press, 1972).

This book is a collection of the author's studies on Mark which have appeared in periodicals. He treats the formation of the Gospel through a critical analysis of A. Trocme's *The*

*Formation of the Gospel According to Mark,* admitting the author's contribution to Marcan studies but taking issue with him in several areas. His study of the Son of Man is of value, as is his exegesis of the Syro-Phoenician woman in 7:24–31.

Dodd, Charles H., *The Apostolic Preaching and Its Development* (London: Hodder, 1936).

This classic work on the primitive kerygma presents an analysis of the Acts of the Apostles with clear presentation on the earliest teachings about Jesus. With this as a background the reader is able to understand better the development that takes place in the origin of the Jesus tradition in the Gospels.

Farmer, William, *The Synoptic Problem: A Critical Analysis* (New York, 1964).

The weight of New Testament scholarship accepts the priority of Mark over Matthew and Luke. What flows from this is the so-called "two-source theory" with the many explanations of the differences and similarities between Matthew, Mark and Luke. Farmer rejects this hypothesis, maintaining a priority for Matthew with his theory of the inter-relatedness of the Synoptics. The opinion of most scholars has not been affected by the theory of Farmer.

Hahn, Ferdinand, *The Titles of Jesus in Christology: Their History in Early Christianity* (London, 1969).

A classic presentation on the titles of Jesus, following the general lines of Tödt. The author analyzes all the instances in which the title appears, manifesting the complexity of the issue as to origin and meaning in the time of Jesus and the Church.

Jeremias, Joachim, *The Parables of Jesus* (New York: Scribner, 1963).

This is a classic study on the parables based upon the historical method. Jeremias is careful to situate the parables in the time of Jesus as well as in the early Church. He carefully delineates what comes from the experience of the Church and what might be traced to Jesus. In recent times this method has been partially enclosed by the works mentioned above by Perrin, Via, Wilder, Crossman, etc.

Jones, Alexander, *The Gospel According to St. Mark* (New York: Sheed and Ward, 1963).

A commentary written for students with a long introduction. The commentary is directed to an analysis of each verse without, however, further comment on the overall theology or meaning of the sections. The book lacks some of the more critical studies of the last decade but offers many helpful insights into the verses of each chapter.

Kahler, Martin, *The So-Called Historical Jesus and the Historic Biblical Christ* (Philadelphia: Fortress, 1964).

A recent English translation of the classical work of the late nineteenth century on the search for the historical Jesus. This work is of interest to the student of the Gospels since it helps explain the interest of the biblical scholars at the turn of the century which has generated much of the development in the historical-critical method.

Kee, Howard C., *Community of the New Age: Studies in Mark's Gospel* (Philadelphia: Westminster, 1976).

This recent study takes an unusual approach to the Gospel. Most studies of the Gospel are based upon an historical approach. More recently scholars are paying attention to the social and cultural factors that influence any literary work. The author tries to combine his background in historical studies in the New Testament with the insights brought by sociology and sociological methods.

Kelber, Werner, *The Kingdom in Mark* (Philadelphia: Fortress, 1974).

This work is a shorter version of the author's doctoral dissertation. Kelber is concerned with the purpose of the Gospel of Mark and proposes that the Gospel has its origin not in Rome but in the north of Israel. It is concerned not so much with the history of Jesus as with the present condition of Christians who must abandon Jerusalem Christianity. The questions of discipleship and suffering have meaning if the believers are today called to move into a future. The Gospel gives the scenario: Jesus suffered and rose, and so the same will be true for the disciples.

Kelber, Werner, *The Passion in Mark* (Philadelphia: Fortress, 1975).

This work is devoted to nine articles on the passion in Mark. The final chapter by the editor is particularly helpful as a summary of many of the Marcan themes related to the passion. The editor relates the findings of the contributors: Donahue, Robbins, Perrin, Dewey, Weeden and Crossan on such topics as the question of a pre-Marcan passion narrative, Christology, the question posed by Weeden of a rival Christology, the issue of the temple, the characters in the narrative and the relationship of the passion account to the rest of the Gospel. This study helps the student to appreciate the development in the analysis of the Marcan passion narrative.

Martin, Ralph, *Mark: Evangelist and Theologian* (Grand Rapids: Zondervan, 1973).

A detailed introduction to the Gospel of Mark treating the Church of the Gospel, Mark's purpose, Christology and contemporary application. The author presents his own thesis for the origin of the Gospel: Mark wished to dispel any doubt as to the true humanity of Jesus and provide a rationale for his death on the cross.

Marxsen, Willi, *Mark the Evangelist* (Nashville: Abingdon, 1969).

This author is a forerunner in the study of redaction criticism. The study is limited in perspective, with attention given to geography in the Gospel and the role of John the Baptist as well as the small apocalypse in chapter 13. This is a modern classic work on Mark.

Nineham, Dennis, *Saint Mark* (Philadelphia: Westminster, 1963).

Also published as a Penguin book, this detailed commentary could be very helpful for the reader interested in greater detail and analysis of the Gospel. Besides the commentary on the verses, the author includes additional background information to help the reader grasp more clearly the assumptions of the author.

Perrin, Norman, *Jesus and the Language of the Kingdom* (Philadelphia: Fortress, 1975).

The association with many colleagues at the University of Chicago influenced Perrin in the study of the New Testament as a literary work. In this book he summarizes the various opinions of scholars with regard to the parables. He admits that the contributions of Jeremias to the study of the question form an historical view but is more impressed with the studies by Wilder, Funk, Via, Crossan and the seminar that met under the auspices of the Society of Biblical Literature. This work is an excellent summary of the opinions of these scholars along with a thorough critique by Perrin.

Perrin, Norman, *A Modern Pilgrim in the New Testament Christology* (Philadelphia: Fortress, 1974).

The author brings the reader up to date on his present positions with regard to such questions as the Son of Man in Mark and its relationship to the use in the other Gospels. Perrin centers much of his study on Mark and summarizes many of the ideas that he has presented in article form.

Perrin, Norman, *The Resurrection According to Matthew, Mark and Luke* (Philadelphia: Fortress, 1976).

This is a comparative study of the various accounts of the resurrection. It is important for the study of Mark since it presents a close analysis of the predictions of the passion as well as some insights into the mind of Mark with regard to the relationship between the passion and the resurrection.

Quesnell, Quentin, *The Mind of Mark* (Rome: Biblical Institute Press, 1969).

This work is an unchanged version of the author's doctoral thesis. It contains a careful exegetical and historical study of 6:52 but is also filled with a wealth of information on the Gospel.

Rohde, John, *Rediscovering the Teaching of the Evangelists* (Philadelphia: Westminster, 1971).

This work is not limited to Mark but includes studies in redaction criticism for each of the Synoptics. A beginner in the study of redaction criticism would benefit immensely from this work.

Schweizer, Edward, *The Good News According to Mark* (Richmond: John Knox, 1970).

The author offers a complete commentary on the Gospel based upon the insights of German scholarship. While he does not deal with specific theological issues or with the concerns of redaction critics, his commentary includes many of the insights of contemporary scholars.

Smith, Morton, *Jesus the Magician* (New York: Harper and Row, 1978).

An interesting, if highly questionable, attempt to relate the magicians of the Jewish-Hellenic milieu to the historical Jesus of Nazareth. The author sees Jesus with the same characteristics as these magicians—hence the title of the book.

Tödt, Howard, *The Son of Man in the Synoptic Tradition* (Philadelphia: Westminster, 1965).

This English translation of the earlier German work (1963) prompted a flood of scholarly works agreeing with, supporting or rejecting the overall analysis of the author's position on the Son of Man. Tödt catalogues the various instances of the title in the Synoptics, and that cataloguing has become classical in the study of the title in the Synoptics. A scholarly work that relates the heavenly authority of Jesus as the Son of Man with the Jesus who acted on earth as the Son of Man.

Trocme, Andre, *The Formation of the Gospel According to Mark* (Philadelphia: Westminster, 1975).

This is a translation of an earlier work which proposes that the Gospel of Mark went through two major revisions. The important element in understanding its origin is to know something of the community which produced it. Trocme is careful to point out the presence in Mark of less sophisticated miracle stories together with more sophisticated legal and ethical matters which would have derived from another milieu. His study of sources and oppositions as well as causes defended by the Gospel offers disputed insights into the Gospel.

Weeden, Theodore J., *Mark: Traditions in Conflict* (Philadelphia: Fortress, 1971).

The author presents the disciples as representing a particular Christology that is judged insufficient by the evangelist. Rightly so, the author sees the Christology as the key to understanding Mark. Whatever position a reader may hold with regard to the central thesis of the work, no one can omit the author's viewpoint from a careful analysis of Mark.

Wrede, William, *The Messianic Secret* (Cambridge: 1971).

This classic work on the Gospel of Mark was the result of an attempt to develop a history of the historical Jesus. Wrede pointed out the tendency in the Gospel for Jesus to demand silence from anyone who knew his identity and thus coined the phrase the "messianic secret." Since then scholars have debated not only the meaning of this secret but its very existence as a secret.